I0469185

DEBARRED THE USE OF ARMS
2nd EDITION

Stephen C. Challis

"No free man shall ever be debarred the use of arms."

Thomas Jefferson

3rd US President

Proposed Virginia Constitution, June, 1776

Dedication Page

To my loving wife Eva, without whose patience and understanding, this book would not have been possible.

Authors note on the Second Edition

Since the publication of 'Debarred the use of Arms' there has been a shift in the policy towards self -defense in the UK. It is small but significant. Judges are looking at self-protection and justification in a new light. As to whether that will lead to more consideration for the victim and less for the criminal remains to be seen. There have also been major events in the US, such as the tragedy at Sandy Hook, which I predicted in the first edition, but take no pleasure in having been proved correct. In this second edition I have updated some of the cases and added illustrations, not available in the first edition.
I trust the reader will approve.

Steve Challis

Debarred the Use of Arms

Foreword

by

Dave Grossman

On April 19th, 1775, an attempt by British troops to confiscate guns from Americans triggered a revolution.

In the war that followed, General Washington didn't use his right to free speech to defeat the British, he shot them. Well, he and several thousand of his fellow armed citizens did.

When the victors of this revolution took power, they established a Constitution and a Bill of Rights. All of these "Rights" were intended to protect the individual citizens from their government.

The first such right was the First Amendment: the right to free speech. The very next thing that the Founding Fathers carved into our national DNA was the Second Amendment: the right to keep and bear arms.

You see, they knew, the Founding Fathers had learned at a tragic cost, that there can be no "rights" unless the citizens can protect themselves from their government. Without the Second Amendment, we would today have only "privileges" granted by the government. And what the government gives, the government can take away.

And yet, as clear and powerful as the Second Amendment and the Bill of Rights may be, there are those in our nation who would twist and distort the original intent of the Founding Fathers and take away that right. These gun control advocates, these gun grabbers, would make us a nation like, well, like England...

The British had no such guarantee. No right to keep and bear arms was established and imprinted indelibly in their national heritage.

Today the citizens of that once proud nation have paid a tragic price, because their government can, *and has*, taken away their right to defend themselves.

The situation in Great Britain today, as well reflected by this book, is so bizarre, that it almost defies belief.

In several cases, those who have used firearms in defense of their homes have been convicted and imprisoned, while the criminals are released. Home invasions are a very common crime, because the criminals know that citizens are unarmed and cannot fight back. Thus creating a pervasive climate of fear, and a citizenry held hostage.

They have truly become the land envisioned in the movie, *A Clockwork Orange.* It is a mad, insane world in which the government acts to protect the criminals, passing law after law in the flawed believe that criminals will obey these laws. But criminals, by definition, will always disobey the law!

British friends of mine who come to visit the US will often go shopping for a set of steak knives, because they can't get them in England!

Steak knives are not (yet) outright banned in England, but the concern for liability is so great that stores won't sell them. What will they try to regulate next? Swords? (No, they already regulated those!) Sticks? Rocks? What will they try to regulate next?

England has tried to license, control, and confiscate all guns for 50 years. This is a small, island nation with complete control of their borders, who have pursued these policies for over 50 years, *and yet gun crime is on the rise!*

And thus the book that you hold in your hands is one of the most important books to be published in recent years, *written by a former British law enforcement officer,* with a vital message that we must read and heed.

If England cannot make gun control work, then there is no way on earth that it will ever work in the US. All England has succeeded in doing is to create one vast "unarmed victim zone." And that is the future of our nation if the gun grabbers have their way!

We are in a battle for the future, soul and safety of our nation, and my good friend Steven Challis in uniquely qualified to give us this message.

Do not just read this book. Study it. Apply it. And pass it on, *with urgency,* to others.

If the gun grabbers have their way, then England is our future. And it is a dark and desperate future, indeed.

LT. COL. DAVE GROSSMAN, U.S. Army (Ret.)

Director, Killology Research Group

www.killology.com

******

Lt. Col. Dave Grossman is a former West Point psychology professor, Professor of Military Science, and an Army Ranger who is the author of *On Killing* (which was nominated for a Pulitzer Prize), *On Combat,* and *Stop Teaching Our Kids to Kill.* Col. Grossman's research was cited by the President of the United States in a national address, and he has testified before the U.S. Senate, the U.S. Congress, and numerous state legislatures.

He has been an expert witness and consultant in state and Federal courts, to include serving on the prosecution team in the Timothy McVeigh, Oklahoma City bombing case. He was involved in counseling, recovery, or court cases in the aftermath of the Jonesboro, Paducah, Springfield, and Littleton school massacres.

He wrote the entry on "Aggression and Violence" in the *Oxford Companion to American Military History,* three entries in the *Academic Press Encyclopedia of Violence, Peace and Conflict* and has presented papers before the national conventions of the American Medical Association, the American Psychiatric Association, the American Psychological Association, and the American Academy of Pediatrics.

Today he is the director of the Killology Research Group, and in the wake of the 9/11 terrorist attacks he is has written and spoken extensively on the terrorist threat, with articles published in the *Harvard Journal of Law and Civil Policy* and many leading law enforcement journals, and he has been on the road almost 300 days a year, training elite military and law enforcement organizations worldwide about the reality of combat.

Contents

Introduction

Debarred the Use of Arms, 2nd Edition

By Stephen C Challis

Introduction

Since the publication of the 1st edition of this book, there have been a number of changes and updates in the law and these have been incorporated. Of course we have also had two more mass shootings, Aurora and Sandy Hook. The debate on the Second Amendment continues and, amazingly Politicians still try to re-interpret the Right to keep and bear arms. President Obama has won a Second term and gun control is back on the radar. In the days following Sandy Hook, this country saw an unprecedented rise in Gun Sales, Senator Diane Feinstein introduced a revamped Assault Weapons Ban and NRA membership exploded at an Initial rate of 8000 per day.

This book is not intended to champion any particular political party or affiliation.

It is designed to give the basic facts as to gun ownership and the rights conferred on

American citizens by the Second Amendment. It is intended to guide the gun owner through the responsibilities of owning and using a firearm. More important than that I hope it will serve as a warning.

On April 18th 1775, celebrated patriot Paul Revere rode from Boston to Lexington to alert the fledgling American Congress that the British were coming. Perhaps if he were able to repeat that famous ride today, his warning would be more specific:

"The British Laws are coming!"

In my home country, the United Kingdom, the sport of recreational pistol shooting has been all but eradicated, along with private handgun ownership, of all but black powder revolvers and long guns, which are very strictly controlled. The United Kingdom had a well-organized gun control lobby which managed, mainly through a process of misinformation, to persuade the UK Government to enact the draconian legislation that achieved this.

Flushed with their success, the UK gun control lobby has now set their sights firmly on the United States as their next target.

However, most Americans feel complacent that such a ban could never happen here, because of The United States Constitution, and more specifically, the Second Amendment.

One of the chinks in the shield of defense, that is The Second Amendment, is the lack of cohesion between the various pro- Second Amendment groups and the infighting that this produces.

This infighting is one of the main causes for the limited success the gun, control lobby is currently enjoying; in effect it is assisting them by splitting the pro- gun lobby. A good example of divide and conquer.

The United States attitude toward gun-control is of course, considerably different from that in the UK at least on the government level. The pro- gun lobby in the UK, much like its American counterpart, feels that they should have the right to own and use guns for legitimate purposes. This is not a view shared by the Police or Government.
To understand this you need to know some of the differences in the two societies.

Firstly, the police force in the United Kingdom is an unarmed one. Police officers on general patrol do not carry firearms. Each division does have a firearms response team, often termed a Tactical Firearms Unit, or T.F.U. These units can be roughly compared to the U.S. SWAT teams, but are not usually as well equipped. One patrol vehicle in each division will have firearms on board, crewed by specially trained officers.

Secondly, the United Kingdom does not have a Constitution, and therefore has no rights guaranteed under it. The Second Amendment is a cornerstone of gun rights in the U.S.A. that many in Britain (including myself) are envious of.

The British Home Office (the department responsible for the police) has since 1920 held the view that personal defense is not a valid reason to own a firearm. Therefore, before the gun- ban was enacted in the UK, the reasons allowable for gun ownership under the regulations were largely confined to sporting and recreation.

I moved to the U.S.A. in 2008 after serving for twenty-one years in the British Police Force. When I joined the force in 1974, Great Britain had gun control but it was limited, and UK citizens could still legally buy and own firearms under those controls, as long as they were not mentally ill, and had no criminal record. Gun ownership was available to all.

There were additional rules on storage and ammunition amounts, as well as a requirement to re-apply for a police permit to buy each additional gun.

The system was not perfect, and in the eyes of US residents, it may even seem draconian. Whilst this may be true, my job as Police Constable in The Aldershot Sub Division in the South of England was, among other duties, to enforce these controls and steer applicants through the process.

At the time, I was also a UK firearms instructor with both the UK National Rifle Association (no connection with the American organization) and The National Small Bore Rifle Association. For a while, I was also secretary of my Divisional Police Pistol club. This meant that I was given a fairly high volume of these enquiries. Looking back, it was an enjoyable learning curve and in addition to ensuring that gun owners understood their responsibilities, I had the opportunity to examine many different types of firearms.

On more than one occasion, I was asked by colleagues to record and make safe weapons brought into the station as found property, or from a crime scene. Sometimes I was asked advice on others. This was in an environment generally hostile to gun ownership.

Now let's put to rest a few myths regarding firearms that were prevalent in the UK, and are not that uncommon here.

Myth 1

Guns are Dangerous!

This is the most often repeated myth, even by gun owners and NRA instructors. Actually, when you think about that statement, it is totally illogical. Guns are tools; they have no mind of their own, no ability to make decisions or distinguish between good and bad.
Grizzly bears, lions, and unstable humans, OK, they are all dangerous, but an inert metal tool? Hardly!

Many inanimate objects can pose a danger in the wrong hands, e.g., a baseball bat, a cigarette lighter, a motor vehicle. I would expect that all but the most extreme gun control freak would agree that point with me.

Common sense also dictates that if, for example, you were to take a weapon, let's say a. 45 cal Thompson Sub Machine gun, load the magazine and rack the slide before laying the gun down on a table. Then walk away leaving it totally alone for 10 years, the weapon would pose no danger to anyone so long as it remained untouched. The gun would only become a danger when someone picked it up from that table.
In other words, the slogan Guns don't kill people, people kill people, is not just a snappy line, it is a statement of fact.

"A sword never kills anybody; it is a tool in the killer's hand."
- Lucius Annaeus Seneca

Myth 2

Gun crime is out of control in America, and it is only in states with the tightest

gun laws that people are reasonably safe.

Actually the opposite is the case. States that have the most gun control laws have the highest crime rates, not just in the U.S.A. but across the world. (We explore this in greater depth in Chapter 2.)

So! If guns are not the problem, what is? Well the answer to this is more complex. To find it we need to look at areas of human psychology, and delve into the mindset of the criminal. In short, we have to decide what makes people kill other people for little or no cause.

Myth 3

Guns only make the situation worse, it's the job of the police to defend us, and they carry out that duty well.

Actually, the police in the U.S.A. do not have a duty to protect, under the Constitution. This fact has been spelled out many times.
The courts have consistently ruled that the police do not have an obligation to protect individuals, only the public in general.

For example, in Warren v. District of Columbia Metropolitan Police Department, 444 A.2d 1 (D.C. App. 1981), the court stated: "Courts have without exception concluded that when a municipality or other governmental entity undertakes to furnish police services, it assumes a duty only to the public at large and not to individual members of the community." In effect this means that you cannot sue the Police if you suffer harm in injury as a result of them neglecting to do what you may perceive as their job.

As I have stated, as a police officer in the United Kingdom, part of my duties involved interviewing applicants who had applied for a gun licenses. (Police Firearm Certificate) Even under the strict gun control measures in the UK it was obvious to me that people that applied for a license were law- abiding and responsible shooters. Few, if any were involved in criminal activity.

They had a desire to use their firearms recreationally and were prepared to comply with regulations to be able to do so.
Those who were not so- minded were most unlikely to go to the expense and Police scrutiny involved in the application process.

In the UK, the criminal use of guns was, unsurprisingly enough, confined to the criminal (it still is both in the UK and U.S.A.) this is a lesson that was ignored in the UK and is also ignored today by the very vocal gun- control lobby in this country. When the UK finally outlawed private handgun ownership, gun crime figures as predicted, went through the roof.

So this is the state of affairs we find existing in the United Kingdom today. The gun control lobby is, in my opinion, a very dangerous movement, in that is advocating policies that have proved to increase gun - related violence in the United Kingdom and will inevitably do so the same in the U.S.A. should they be implemented. The facts are plain and clear. You need not take my word for it the data is public record for any researcher to find. The arguments are not new, but more of this is in chapter 5.
The Marquis Cesar Beccaria, an Italian born in Milan in 1738, was a celebrated criminologist, philosopher, and politician, who in 1764 published a treatise on Crime and Punishment.

It is unknown whether or not James Madison had actually ever read the document, but certainly he would have been aware of it. The Document was well known to the other Founders. John Adams quoted from the work while addressing the Jury in defense of the British troops at the infamous Boston Massacre trial. But there is no doubt Madison would have agreed with the feisty Italian's view on gun control advocates.

Beccaria had little time for gun banners. This is clear from a paper he wrote at the time.

"False is the idea ... that would take fire from men because it burns, and water because one may drown in it ... The laws that forbid the carrying of arms are laws of such a nature. They disarm those only who are neither inclined nor determined to commit crimes.

Can it be supposed that those who have the courage to violate the most sacred laws of humanity, the most important of the code, will respect the less important and arbitrary ones, which can be violated with ease and impunity, and which, if strictly obeyed, would put an end to personal liberty.

Such laws make things worse for the assaulted and better for the assailants; they serve rather to encourage than to prevent homicides."

Thomas Jefferson was also aware of Beccaria's work and copied the above passage in his own work, Commonplace *Book.*

I have no hesitation in following suit. This 250- year- old document is as valid today as when it was written. If it's good enough for Adams and Jefferson, then it draws no argument from me.

The logic that the Marquis used in his statement would clearly be understood by Gun owners in the 21st Century. It appears that as long as people have owned guns, there have been others who have wanted to take them away.

The 18th century equivalents of the Brady group were using the same arguments then, as are being rehashed now.

At the time Beccaria wrote those words, America was still a collection of colonies with a mood of resentment that would reach it crescendo at Lexington and Concorde in 1775.

By reading this book, you have already demonstrated an open mind and a desire to understand the dangers of the restrictions that a ban on firearms would have on your ability to defend yourself and family. Since moving to the U.S.A., I have watched the same arguments creep into the debate on gun -control here. In this book, I have attempted to clear away some of the falsehoods and baseless arguments that have emerged in this country.

This book may serve as a warning from history. Former British Prime Minister Margaret Thatcher coined the phrase that Britain and the U.S.A. have a special relationship. That is true. Similar problems exist in both countries and we both work peaceably to resolve them.

We do, however, have totally opposite views on gun ownership; it would be naïve for anyone to think that the riots and lawless behavior currently plaguing the UK and Europe cannot happen here.
Not only can and has it happened but we can actually see it every day manifested in the high crime rates in states and cities that have

the strictest gun laws.

Whether the U.S.A. goes the way of Britain, or remains a bastion of firearms rights, is in the hands of her people. I make no apologies to anyone who may be upset by the facts herein. This book does however provide the reader with more than enough evidence on which to make a call.

So let's begin the journey.

Chapter 1

<u>The Second Amendment</u>

The Second Amendment is actually the second of 10 amendments to the United States Constitution. Penned by Founding Father James Madison, these 10 amendments are known collectively as the Bill of Rights. That is rights that set down the cornerstone of American democracy. As such they were, in effect set in stone and cannot be overruled changed, or watered down, except by a two-thirds majority vote in the Senate, an unlikely occurrence in the U.S.A.

So The Bill of Rights means exactly what it says, no more, and no less.

Speaking in Congress on June 11th 1789, Massachusetts Representative Fisher Ames put it thus,

"Mr. Madison has introduced his long expected amendments. They are the fruit of much Labor and Research.

He has hunted up all the grievances and complaints of newspapers, all the articles of convention and the small talk of their debates.
It contains a Bill of Rights. The Right of enjoying property, of changing the Government at Pleasure, freedom of the press, of conscience, of juries, exemption from the general warrants...Oh I had forgot the right of the people to keep and bear arms. "

Well! Representative Ames can be forgiven the momentary lapse. Politicians ever since have been trying to enjoy a similar lapse. But, as stated these amendments were presented to congress after much research and listening to the electorate. Another trait often lacking in today's society.

James Madison knew only too well the necessity of including a firearms amendment. That is why it is number 2 in the list. For having been freed from the repression of a British government regime that had to control its citizens.

The new congress had no desire to inflame the populace by replacing one tyrannical rule with another.

"A free people ought not only to be armed and disciplined, but they should have sufficient arms and ammunition to maintain a status of independence from any who might attempt to abuse them, which would include their own government."
- George Washington

Madison realized that any constitution had to guarantee its citizens freedom to live, work, and worship how they pleased. Sure there had to be regulation to ensure law and order, but regulations were to be kept to a minimum and the power the government had was to be firmly left in the hands of the people.

An attempt by the British at Concord and Lexington in 1775 to seize arms from the colonial arsenal had spawned the whole War of Independence. A fact not lost on the shrewd Madison or the newly constituted Congress of The United States.

The new Constitution would be designed to ensure that no national government would be able to disarm the population again.

Madison knew that such an amendment was a necessity to get the agreement of the country as a whole, wherein ratification was concerned. He and Congress also knew that such an amendment needed to be unequivocal. It had to be in the clearest possible terms and impervious to any legal or political tampering. So far, they have succeeded. In fact, the careful wording of the Second Amendment has so far frustrated even the most anti- gun politicians.

So why were the people so adamant that they needed to keep their guns? The simple answer is self-protection.

Protection for themselves and their families from danger posed from whom we now call Native Americans, from wild and dangerous animals and most of all they feared a future government imposing an agenda by force. A disarmed population is far easier to control.

The people of the New World, as it was known in Europe, were in no mood to compromise. So the right of every citizen to keep and bear arms was required and the Congress duly delivered.

OK! Let's look at the Second Amendment and dissect it.

"A well- regulated militia being necessary to the security of a Free State. The right of the People to keep and bear arms shall not be infringed."

The first line gives the reasoning behind the amendment. The writers are stating that an armed militia is essential if a state is to remain free. All citizens had agreed that arms were necessary to make certain that your freedom and safety remained secure in the United States of America where they lived.

So what of the well-regulated militia? Well! Lawyers have chewed this one over many times depending on which side they are representing. In effect, the amendment says:

As a free state we require an armed citizenry to ensure our security.
WW2 Japanese naval commander, Admiral Yamamoto realized this when he is famously reported to have pronounced,
"You cannot invade America. There would be a rifle behind every blade of grass."
The term militia may be translated as citizen soldiers.
However the original definition can be found in the *The Militia Act of 1792.*

The relevant part of which reads,

" Be it enacted by the Senate and House of Representatives of the United States of America, in Congress assembled, That each and every free able-bodied white male citizen of the respective States, resident therein, who is or shall be of age of eighteen years, and under the age of forty-five years (except as is herein after excepted) shall severally and respectively be enrolled in the militia, by the Captain or Commanding Officer of the company, within whose bounds such citizen shall reside, and that within twelve months after the passing of this Act."

Therefore when trying to decide what Madison meant by the term, Militia, it is more relevant to read the definition as it existed then. The term may have been modified and altered over the last 200 years, but that is irrelevant.

The term Militia as used in the language of the Second Amendment has to refer to the meaning that was correct then at the time the *Militia Act of 1792* was written.

Although this is an obvious view to take, it is not one shared by the Brady Group who prefers to improve on the original definition and impose a modern definition, rather than stick with the 1792 original. It is not hard to see why.

If every citizen were a militiaman then the Second Amendment would apply to everyone. Not a position any self respecting gun banner would relish. So what of the modern definition?

Currently the US legal code states;
"Militia refers to a body of citizens armed and trained by the state for military service apart from the regular armed forces. It is composed of physically fit civilians eligible by law for military service. It characterizes a military force recruited directly from civilians who would not otherwise be liable to serve in a state's regular armed forces.

It can also refer to unorganized military force drawn from within a civilian population and which has taken up arms. For example, in modern Somalia the armed followers of different warlords have been characterized as militias. The definition has been under attack and interpretation in recent years."

Hmm! Not much better but at least the anti gun brigade can try to use this interpretation as a lever to at least ban some people from owning guns.

Well! Sorry guys, not any longer. The Supreme Court ruled in the case Heller v District of Columbia 2008 as follows.

"(1) The Second Amendment protects an individual right to possess a firearm unconnected with service in a militia, and to use that arm for traditionally lawful purposes, such as self-defense within the home. Pp. 2–53.

(a) The Amendment's prefatory clause announces a purpose, but does not limit or expand the scope of the second part, the operative clause. The operative clause's text and history demonstrate that it connotes an individual right to keep and bear arms. Pp. 2–22.

(b) The prefatory clause comports with the Court's interpretation of the operative clause. The "militia" comprised all males physically capable of acting in concert for the common defense. Therefore every male citizen is a member of the militia, at least as far as the Constitution goes."

OK! I hear you say, very eloquent, but what exactly does it mean?
Basically the Court dismissed any notion that the Second Amendment meant anything other than what it said. The right to keep and bear arms is an individual right, not connected with service in any Militia.

As my childhood cartoon hero Dick Dastardly would most defiantly have said

"Drat and double Drat."

Actually the same misinterpretation of the second amendment is prevalent in the term *well regulated*. In the 18th Century this term meant well trained and, not the current meaning of subject to rules and regulations.

The Brady group had been thwarted again. But they, like the tenacious aforementioned Dick Dastardly would be unlikely to give up. They will continue to attack the Second Amendment and try to introduce gun control legislation. This would probably be in a piecemeal way via States and liberal city administrations. This was the strategy that worked so well in the UK.

The NRA is well aware of this strategy and will no doubt continue the assault on these enclaves, hoping to emulate their success in places such as Chicago and Washington.

No doubt the Supreme Court ruling will not be the end of the matter, but it does seem clear that there is unlikely to be an identical challenge in the foreseeable future.

OK! Back to the wording of the Second Amendment

The second line, "The right of the people to keep and bear arms," affirms that this is an existing right already in evidence. The first sentence is merely an explanation of why this right exists.

The final line, *"Shall not be infringed,"* would appear to be self- evident. It states that no legislation can be enacted that in any way restricts gun ownership. Unfortunately most gun- control advocates seem incapable of comprehending the phrase which is why the courts have to continually remind them.

So having written the right to own a gun into the Constitution, our Founding Fathers moved on to forge a new nation.

America is almost unique in enshrining the right of the people to own guns into law.

This being said there are restrictions on gun ownership in this country. The most obvious pertain to age and mental state. Further the convicted felon also loses his rights under the Second Amendment. So there are limits placed on gun ownership in the U.S.A.

Principally at the federal level these are contained in The Gun Control Act 1968 which lists prohibited persons. Next we will examine these restrictions and how they affect gun ownership in the United States.

The strongest reason for people to retain the right to keep and bear arms is, as a last resort, to protect themselves against tyranny in government."
- Thomas Jefferson

Chapter 2

US Gun Control Measures

The Second Amendment, as we have seen, gives all citizens the right to keep and bear arms. In recent years, more than one academic has put forth the point of view that, taken literally, this would mean any US Citizen, including felons, mental patients, and young children could own and use guns. Certainly this is an aspect often pointed out by the Brady Group in their relentless efforts to have the Amendment replaced or cancelled. Common sense, (an increasingly rare commodity in American politics since Thomas Paine's book of the same name, first hit the news stands in 1776) dictates that there have to be some clarification made to the law.

The first limits were imposed arbitrarily by the courts and were accepted without much argument.

No lawyer would dare suggest that a mentally unstable person should be allowed to carry a gun, and equally it may not be a good idea to allow a person convicted of murder or armed robbery to possess them either.

Unfortunately, these restrictions, once accepted, were expanded upon by some states to, in effect, stretch the envelope, to include blacks, freed slaves, Catholics, immigrants, in fact anyone distrusted by the Authorities. So the first federal law was put into place. Its implementation was fought over by both sides but finally it made it onto the statute books.

The Gun Control Act 1968

The Gun Control Act 1968 was the first real challenge to the Second Amendment This bill, like similar ones in England followed the fear and anger that swept the country following a tragedy. In the US it followed the assassinations of President John F Kennedy (Dallas 1963) Robert Kennedy (Los Angeles 1968) and Martin Luther King (Memphis 1968) as well as the Civil rights protests of the mid 60s.

The Act grew out of perceived groundswell of support for tough gun- control laws; this reached unprecedented levels, thanks to a largely liberal media.

On June 6, the day after the Kennedy assassination, Johnson signed the Safe Streets and Crime Control Act, but was not happy with what he deemed to be the law's weak provisions.

President Johnson had proposed gun-control measures every year since becoming president, following the assassination of President Kennedy. Johnson also appeared on national television imploring Congress to pass a new and tougher gun- control law that banned mail order and out-of-state sales of long guns and ammunition. He pleaded to Congress in a letter "in the name of sanity, in the name of safety, and in the name of an aroused nation, to give America the gun-control law it needs." On June 24, President Johnson again addressed the country, calling for mandatory national gun- registration and licenses for every gun owner.

In those days, the anti- gun charge was led by Johnson, Senator Edward Kennedy, and Former NASA Astronaut Col John Glenn, a boyhood hero of mine, who I am sad to say showed very ill- conceived views. All three, lets say, misguidedly, believed that guns were the primary source of violent crime, citing the ease with which assassins Lee Harvey Oswald (JFK) and Sirhan Sirhan (Robert Kennedy), obtained their guns.

Under the GCA, firearms possession by certain categories of individuals is prohibited.

1.   Anyone who has been convicted in a federal court of a crime punishable by imprisonment for a term exceeding one year, excluding crimes of imprisonment that are related to the regulation of business practices.
2.   Anyone who has been convicted in a state court of a crime punishable by imprisonment for a term exceeding two years, excluding crimes that are related to the regulation of business practices.
3.   Anyone who is a fugitive from justice.
4.   Anyone who is an unlawful user of, or addicted to, any controlled substance.

5.   Anyone who has been adjudicated as a mental defective or who has been committed to a mental institution

6.   Any alien illegally or unlawfully in The United States, or an alien admitted to the United States under a non-immigrant visa. Legal, non-immigrant aliens may possess guns if they have a current, valid hunting license.

7.   Anyone who has been discharged under dishonorable conditions from the United States armed forces.

8.   Anyone who, having been a citizen of the United States, has renounced his or her citizenship.

9.   Anyone that is subject to a court order that restrains the person from harassing, stalking, or threatening an intimate partner or child of such intimate partner. (Added 1996)

10.   Anyone who has been convicted of a misdemeanor crime of domestic violence (added in 1996 by the Domestic Violence Offender Gun Ban, or "Lautenberg Amendment.")

Additionally, 18 USC 922(x) generally prohibits persons under 18 from possessing handguns or handgun ammunition, with certain exceptions for employment, target practice, education, and a handgun possessed while defending the home of the juvenile or a home in which they are an invited guest.

A person who is under indictment or information for a crime punishable by imprisonment for a term exceeding one year cannot lawfully receive a firearm. Such person may continue to lawfully possess firearms obtained prior to the indictment or information.

Although this law was heavily criticized by some including the NRA, most Americans were of the view that these restrictions would not prevent law abiding citizens from possessing firearms for both self defense and sporting purposes.

In England the equivalent legislation was the 1968 Firearms Act, which consolidated the existing legislation and put restrictions on shotguns and ammunition, but more of this in the next chapter.

Having got the 1968 gun -control law passed in the US, the anti gun groups set out to tighten the noose even further.

The Brady Handgun Violence Prevention Act of 1993

The Brady Handgun Violence Prevention Act of 1993 was introduced by Sara and James Brady, and named after James, who received a serious wound during the attempted assassination of President Reagan while he was serving as press secretary under him.

The Act signed into law by anti- gun President William Clinton, created a national background check system to prevent firearms sales to prohibited persons."

(Note here, if you want to get a bill through Congress give it a name that makes it difficult to oppose.

The same tactics were used across the Atlantic in the UK with the 2006 Violent Crime Reduction Act, which effectively banned the private ownership of modern handguns for any purpose. But more on the UK's problems later.

FFL System

The Gun Control Act 1968 mandated the licensing of individuals and companies engaged in the business of selling firearms. This provision effectively prohibited the direct mail order of firearms (except antique firearms) by consumers, and mandated that anyone who wanted to buy a gun from a source other than a private individual must do so through a federally licensed firearms dealer.

The Act also banned unlicensed individuals from acquiring handguns outside their state of residence.

The interstate purchase of long guns (rifles and shotguns) was not impeded by the act, so long as the seller was federally licensed, and such a sale was allowed by both the state of purchase and the state of residence.

Private sales between residents of two different states were also prohibited without going through a licensed dealer, except in the case of a buyer holding a Curio & Relic license, purchasing a firearm that qualified as a curio or relic.

These were listed by the BATF, but generally refer to historic weapons at least 50 years old.

There are, of course, exceptions, including fully automatic weapons. As the years go by, I would expect further restrictions from the BAFT to take into account the passage of time, most likely a raising of the limit to guns of 75 years of age or older.

Private sales between unlicensed individuals who are residents of the same state are allowed under federal law so long as such transfers do not violate other existing federal and state laws. While current law mandates that a background check be performed if the seller has a federal firearms license, private parties living in the same state are not required to perform such checks under federal law. State laws, however, can prohibit such sales.

A person who does not have a Federal Firearms License may not be *in the business* of buying or selling firearms. Individuals with a C&R, buying and selling firearms without a federal license must be doing so from their own personal collection.

The Gun- Control Act forbids sales of all firearms by federally licensed dealers to persons under the age of 18, and sales of handguns by federally licensed dealers to persons under the age of 21.

Curiously, the government feels that our young soldiers can be trusted to use handguns to defend themselves and the country, but not to have them to defend their families in the U.S.A.

So we are now seeing that far from being a nation where the people are trigger-happy cowboys, Owning and using a gun is actually pretty well regulated under the law of the United States.

Even so there are those who continue to push for stronger control, and politicians who seem more than happy to oblige.

The answer to this attack on the Second Amendment was an organization that would eventually lead a fight for the gun owner. That organization was formed in 1871. Again it was unique to the U.S.A.

THE BIG PICTURE

So, let's look at gun control on a global
scale, a look back into history, to see how
gun control has worked out beyond these
shores. The statistics are sobering, to say the
least.

In 1929, the Soviet Union established gun-
control. From 1929 to 1953, about 20
million dissidents, now unable to defend
themselves, were rounded up and
exterminated.

In 1911, Turkey established gun- control.
From 1915 to 1917, 1.5 million Armenians,
also with no means of defending themselves,
were rounded up and exterminated.

Germany established gun- control in 1938
and from 1939 to 1945, under the direction
of Nazi leader, Adolf Hitler, who ordered
the confiscation of all privately owned
firearms. The authorities then had little
problem rounding up a total of 13 million
Jews and others who were unable to defend
themselves. They were shipped to camps
and exterminated.

China established gun control in 1935, effectively disarming their population from 1948 to 1952. Result 20 million political dissidents, again unable to defend themselves, they were rounded up and exterminated.

Guatemala established gun- control in 1964. From 1964 to 1981, 100,000 Mayan Indians, unable to defend themselves, were rounded up and exterminated.

Uganda established gun- control in 1970. From 1971 to 1979, 300,000 Christians, unable to defend themselves, were rounded up and exterminated.

Cambodia established gun control in 1956. From 1975 to 1977, one million educated people, unable to defend themselves, were rounded up, and exterminated. Anyone other than me, see a pattern here?

In the 20th Century a total of 56 million people were exterminated by their governments after having being disarmed. Faced with these alarming statistics is it little wonder that Americans will not surrender their arms easily.

So, the evidence is irrefutable that governments who desire total control of their populations will ensure that they are disarmed first.

Now, before the left wing and liberal extremists get all riled up and start their rhetoric, let me be crystal clear.

I am not suggesting that the present administration or even any future one, would ever take this course in This country, but the facts do show why Americans are reluctant to give up their guns.

It is true that the aforementioned examples are extreme ones. However, we should in my opinion, seriously question any attempts by the government to register and ban certain weapons. Remember once minor restrictions are implemented, more restrictive ones are easier to impose. I know that first hand and so does The Brady Group.

Remember all reviews of gun control statistics in this country totally debunk the idea that gun- control is about safety.

In the U.S.A. data shows overwhelmingly that states with the toughest gun- control legislation also have the highest gun- crime rates.

This is despite claims by the Brady group and other anti gun organizations. The reason is fairly clear, but you have to look for it.

My local police chief told me in 2011 that interviews with arrested felons in Kentucky showed that they were very concerned about facing armed citizens during burglaries. Often they would try to target homes they knew, or thought unlikely to be armed.

In fact, let's say that you, as a governor of a US state introduce a total ban on keeping a gun in your home. You are, in fact telling the felons of that state that you have removed their one big fear in committing a crime. This was certainly the situation in the UK, when following the ban, gun crime soared.

Ok! So why does the gun-control lobby insist on trying to disarm us? Well it is true that gun accidents are a cause for concern.

A loaded firearm left casually around the home, forgetting to secure your weapon when practicing on the range or carelessness in handling, or even when talking about guns, when hunting and in the view of the public can give ammunition to the anti gun brigade. All contribute to the myth of an out- of- control gun culture.

The NRA, and most shooting clubs and organizations, continually hammer firearm safety. But the gun owner who simply buys a gun for protection and who puts it in a drawer and forgets it, is also a risk.

Before we go any further lets put the gun accident rate into perspective.

Every year in the U.S.A. 500 children die from accidental drowning in home swimming pools, as opposed to 40 who die from gun- related accidents.

There are 5 million households with swimming pools in the U.S.A. and approximately 43 million with guns. Statistically you are 5 times more likely to die at the hands of a doctor than by a gun. But we all still trust doctors and seek attention for our medical problems.

And we still swim happily in our backyard pools with our children.

Sarah Brady and her group seem unable to grasp this, so, sorry, Sarah, the facts do not support the need for more restrictive legislation, unless of course the Brady group also advocates outlawing doctors and swimming pools. And what about the death rate from motor accidents?

So! Moving on from accidents, what about criminals? Well maybe we should start by looking at the definition of criminal. A criminal or felon is someone who breaks the law. It is therefore difficult to see the logic that making a law will force a lawbreaker to obey that particular law. We have already seen clearly that it will certainly make his or her life easier. Incidentally, states that have a concealed- carry law have, on average a 13% lower murder rate than those without. A fact not unnoticed by the States who all (except Illinois) had passed such legislation by August 2011.

You won't see this data on the U.S. evening news or hear politicians disseminating this information. They have a different agenda. I can say this both as an ex- police officer and as a former politician, myself.

A Politician has one driving force, to get elected. Many do believe passionately in the cause of their particular convictions and that is to be applauded, but to achieve their aspirations they still need to garner and obtain votes. This is done by trying to represent as large a cross section of the electorate as possible. No easy task.

While campaigning in the UK for the 2004 general election I was asked at a town hall meeting for my view on fox hunting (a contentious issue in England). I replied that my party had no policy either for or against but felt it a matter for individual conscience, a true politician's answer but my formidable lady questioner was not to be put off. She said pointedly, "Thank you Mr. Challis, I did not ask what your party's policy was. I asked what you, personally, believe."

My reply, much to the horror of my campaign manager, was, "Well! Personally I am in favor of fox hunting as an efficient way of controlling predators."

The lady thanked me, and both she and her companion got up and left.

This may have ruffled my campaign team, but I felt she deserved a straight, not a political answer, I think that too many politicians do not feel that way.

Both The NRA and Brady Campaign group publish lists of recommended candidates before elections, based on the candidate's record on supporting or opposing gun legislation. A review of these candidates' records will furnish the public with the information needed to support them or not.

A candidate with a solid record of voting for anti- gun legislation is unlikely to change his or her view, no matter what they may say publically. Likewise, a solid supporter of the Second Amendment is also likely to continue defending it.

Do not fall into the trap of assuming that only Republican candidates support gun-rights. This issue crosses party lines, and many high profile Democrats are steadfast defenders of the Second Amendment. This book is not the proper forum to identify these politicians. The readers can do that research themselves. But remember, the fight for the right to keep and bear arms starts at the ballot box.

If you cannot be bothered to vote, then, in all honesty, you do not have any reason to protest if anti- gun lawmakers take away your guns.

Guns in the hands of honest citizens save lives and property, and, yes, gun-control laws adversely affect the law-abiding citizen. Unfortunately they affect *only* the law-abiding citizen. If American gun owners want to keep their guns and ensure that gun-control does not become widespread then they need to act. In the next chapter, we will explore how America is fighting back.

"These Sarah Brady types must be educated to understand that because we have an armed citizenry, that a dictatorship has not happened in America. These anti-gun fools are more dangerous to liberty than street criminals or foreign spies."

~Theodore Haas, Dachau Survivor

Chapter 3

The National Rifle Association

The NRA traces its origins to the 1870s, when two former Union Army officers, Colonel William Conant Church and General George Wingate, formed the National Rifle Association to foster marksmanship. The NRA was chartered in the state of New York on November 17, 1871. Another well-known Civil War veteran, General Ambrose Burnside, served as the group's first president. Burnside had been a U.S. Senator and governor of Rhode Island. Although he lobbied very effectively for funding, he was not otherwise actively involved in the fledgling group, and resigned within a year.

Through the founders' efforts, the state of New York granted the NRA $25,000 to create a practice ground on a 100- acre lot on Long Island. The Creedmoor Range opened there in 1873, and hosted the Irish Rifle Association in a two-entrant international shooting competition held the next year.

The event drew 8,000 spectators. Even in those early days, however, the NRA faced anti-gun sentiment in the cities, and in 1892 the land grant was rescinded and the range was moved to Sea Girt, New Jersey.

New York governor, Alonzo Cornell was predicting a long age of peace, and in a cost cutting measure he cut the NRA's funding in 1880. However, technological innovations and worrying events overseas soon made weapons training in the US relevant again.

Dutch South African farmers were demonstrating the effectiveness of new, highly accurate rifles against the disciplined and regular British Army in the Boer War, which led to a renewed interest in marksmanship and military preparedness in the British Empire and in America.

A revitalized NRA began setting up programs at colleges and military schools beginning in 1903; within three years, there were more than 200 young men competing at the shooting contest in New Jersey.

NRA headquarters was moved to Washington, D.C. in 1907.

According to OSHA, Gray Davidson's informative book, *Under Fire,* the NRA persuaded Congress and the War Department to sell surplus military arms, and also ammunition, to NRA-sponsored shooting clubs.

Later, this arrangement led to *free* supplies. A remnant of this exists today in the Civilian Marksmanship Program, which allows for the purchase of surplus military weapons such as the M1 Garand, by US citizens, without the need to transfer via an FFL.

Between World War I and World War II, 200,000 rifles were reportedly distributed *at cost* to NRA members, whose ranks were rapidly increasing. The NRA also received federal money and assistance from the US Army for its shooting competitions during this time. The military and government were happy, and the ethos of the Second Amendment to maintain a strong militia was alive and well.

During these early years, the NRA did not campaign in support of the Second Amendment. Quite simply, there was no need.

The country, as a whole, was very supportive of the right of Americans to defend their selves and no politician would have dreamt of campaigning to change that.

Among the vehicles of communication was the group's flagship publication, *The American Rifleman,* published sporadically at first and later gaining a large and regular readership. Subscription to American Rifleman is now one of a choice of publications included with every NRA membership.

In the 1930s a huge NRA letter- writing campaign helped temper one wave of gun control sentiment ensuring that the National Firearms Act of 1934 would extend only to regulating machine guns and sawed-off shotguns.

In 1938, the NRA supported provisions to limit the sale of guns across state lines, and to prevent the sale of guns to fugitives and convicted felons.

At the dawn of World War II, the NRA collected 7,000 guns to aid Great Britain's defense.

When the United States was drawn into the war, the NRA offered its facilities and encouraged its members to guard factories.

In the postwar years, the NRA focused on hunting issues, developing a pioneering hunter education program with the state of New York. The Association also began a program for instructing policemen in marksmanship; it would introduce the country's only national law enforcement certification program in 1960.

Membership in the NRA reached nearly 300,000 and the association employed a staff 140 in the 1950s. A new NRA shooting range, Camp Perry, had been constructed in Ohio on the Lake Erie shore, and during this time, it became home to the NRA's National Matches. The U.S. government supplied $3 million a year, along with the use of 5,000 troops a year for these tournaments.

Of course it was not to last. The gun- control lobby had found a voice and opposition was building to such government aid.

Inevitably close association between the NRA and government was challenged; Senator Edward Kennedy attempted to cut off the financial aid in the late 1960s and routinely fought NRA- backed bills in Congress throughout his career.

Kennedy could be said to be the founder of the modern anti gun movement in the US. At this time, the membership of the NRA also began to realize that there were dangers in being too closely aligned with the government and as a result, the organization, in my opinion, became more politically active.

The opposite was also true, with more anti-gun members of congress pressing for the government to distance itself from the NRA.

In 1973, the NRA launched a new magazine, *The American Hunter*, addressing hunting issues only. This was designed to strengthen the influence of the organization as being representative of all shooting sports.

Two years later, with anti- gun storm clouds already on the horizon; it formed the Institute for Legislative Action (ILA), designed specifically as a lobby for Second Amendment rights.

The Association's Legislative Action Division primary goal was to disseminate information to its members regarding pending gun- control legislation and to challenge anti- gun legislation that infringed the second amendment. A task for which has been very successful.

The NRA.ILA was headed by Harlon Bronson Carter, a controversial Texan who had been indicted for his involvement in the shooting murder of a Mexican youth, for which he was convicted and later cleared.

Concurrent with Carters tenure the NRA was evolving and changing, a rift was developing between those supporting the single issue of Second Amendment rights and those hoping to broaden the scope of the NRA. It culminated, at the NRA national convention of 1977 in Cincinnati Ohio.

Led by Carter, the so-called 'hard-liners' took over the convention in what has since become known as the 'Cincinnati Revolt. The hard liners saw a real threat to the Second Amendment, and were determined that the organization would not sit idly by while the government took away their rights.

It seemed as is the spirit of Texas, forged at the Alamo in 1836 was still strong in the blood of its fiery 20th century son. No doubt, Crockett, Travis, and Bowie were cheering, up in heaven.

Carter and his supporters were fervently opposed to any form of gun control, and wrested control of the NRA from its existing leaders, whose concerns seem to be limited to sportsmanship and environmentalism, turning the NRA into a single- issue gun lobby. Carter was named executive vice-president, the most powerful position in the organization. From then on the NRA became a force strong enough to take on the gun- control lobby and address the issue of increasing violent crime in this country.

The NRA called for more prisons, tougher sentences, and more law enforcement officers. However, the Association continued to struggle with public relations issues and managed to alienate certain law enforcement groups.

Congressman John Dingell, an NRA board member, had called the U.S. Department of Alcohol, Tobacco, and Firearms (BATF) a 'jackbooted group of fascists' in one of the group's promotional films.

This alarmed some of the moderates in the organization, and gave fuel to the Brady groups' agenda in 1981. The NRA repeated the rhetoric from Dingle in a 1995 fundraising letter. This prompted former president George Bush to rescind his life membership.

In October 1997 nine firearms manufacturers, including Smith & Wesson, announced they were voluntarily adding child safety locks to their products.

This unexpected break from NRA policy was prompted by a litigious climate that had anti- gun city administrations such as those of Chicago and New Orleans filing lawsuits similar to the ones that had been launched against the cigarette industry.

In doing this the gun makers risked a boycott by NRA members who opposed compromise of any kind. According to *Newsweek,* the publicly traded Sturm, Ruger and Co Inc, firm had faced such a boycott earlier in the decade after it had come out in favor of limiting high capacity ammo clips for assault weapons.

In 1997, in the face of such challenges, the NRA began publishing *The American Guardian,* designed to appeal to a more general audience, with less emphasis on technical subjects and more on self-defense and sporting use of firearms.

This helped calm the furor stirred up by the Brady campaign. During which membership of the NRA, having after reached 3.5 million, had fallen by about a million in the mid-1990s. Still, in 1998 the group held the largest convention in its history, attracting 41,000 attendees. In the same year, the NRA elected as its president, the actor, Charlton Heston, perhaps best known for his performance as Moses in the epic film, *The Ten Commandments.* Most NRA members remember Heston's stirring, *From My cold dead hands* speech at the 129th NRA convention on May 20th 2000, in Charlotte, North Carolina.

Another famous actor, Tom Selleck, appeared in a new round of magazine advertising for the NRA. He is now a director within the organization.

In the late 1990s, following several highly publicized incidents of violence involving guns among American teenagers, some polls indicated that 70 to 80 percent of Americans favored stricter gun control laws.

However, *Newsweek* reported, the fear of political retaliation from the NRA killed a new round of gun- control bills in June 1999.

NRA membership climbed again late in the decade. By May 2000, at the time Charlton Heston was rallying supporters at Charlotte. The Association reported 3.7 million members were now fighting challenges to the right to bear arms.

The NRA is probably the only reason that the Second Amendment was not repealed years ago.

According to the latest figures there are approximately 80 million gun owners in America with a combining total of 258 million guns. In contrast to those figures, there are only approximately 4 million that are members of the National Rifle Association. Despite this, the NRA has kept up the fight for the rights of all gun owners since its inception in 1871.

The attempts by Congress and state legislators to strike down the Second Amendment have been relentless. At each attempt to introduce gun restrictions, the NRA's legal wing, the Institute for Legislative Affairs, has stood against them and won the day. It remains to be seen if this trend will continue.

Only last year, the landmark case of "Heller v District of Columbia" challenging the Washington, DC handgun ban was decided in favor of gun owners forcing the District to back down. Similar gun- ban, laws were hastily re-thought when the NRA filed lawsuits against those states concerned.

These states, however, were slow to accept defeat, and many replaced outright bans with complex restrictions on gun ownership, designed to make it difficult to obtain a gun for use in self-defense. These restrictions included high fees, waiting periods, excessive security arrangements and a question on reasons the applicant needed a gun. Most of these restrictions clearly breached the second amendment and resulted in further writs being filed by the NRA against the various administrations.

The nationwide concealed- carry permit laws also owe their existence to the NRA, as do the rights to keep weapons in the home for self- defense. In fact the states that stubbornly refused to implement Concealed Carry laws were systematically targeted and brought into line until by 2011 only Illinois remained. And its legislators are aware that an election is looming in 2012.

As a Police Officer for 21 years in the United Kingdom, I have seen gun rights first restricted then obliterated, in my home country.
This was done using the same arguments that the anti- gun politicians are now using in the U.S.A. The UK currently has the most restrictive gun ownership laws in Europe and of course one of the highest gun crime rates.

The right of self-defense in the UK is also virtually non-existent. Even today you are more likely to be arrested for injuring an intruder than the perpetrator is for breaking into your home.

The total ban on handguns was introduced by the British government to quell the anger following a tragedy at Dunblane. This has, of course, had a number of effects. The UK

Olympic shooting teams have been prevented from owning or training in the UK, effectively eliminating any chance of serious competitiveness. The sport of competitive shooting has been all but eliminated. The ban, of course, had absolutely no effect on the reduction of crime; in fact statistics from the UK Home Office show the opposite is true. We will explore the situation in the UK more fully in the next chapter.

Approximately twenty years ago, the state governments in the US started going after companies that made inexpensive firearms. They did this by focusing on the melt temperature of the metal that the gun was made from.

Elitists heavily criticized these guns and called them' unsafe and 'not required for a free society. The phrase *Saturday night special* fell into common use.
The reasons were more to do with commercial protectionism than any real concern over safety. In the U.S.A., major gun manufacturers saw their profits under threat and mounted a campaign to eliminate competition by questioning the effectiveness and safety of less expensive guns.

Most gun owners disagreed, and so did the NRA. The NRA defended the manufacture of inexpensive guns when it was not popular to do so, and for that reason, we have companies like Cobra Industries of today. They bring self- defense to those who can't afford a higher quality and much more expensive option.

Today Internet blogs are still full of self-appointed experts decrying these guns and advising owners to throw them away and buy a decent Colt or Glock, but give no answer to the question, " what if the would be gun owner does not have the funds to do that?" I suppose the advice from these- so called experts would have to be, "well, start saving, and try not to get shot until you can afford one."
Unlike most of the Internet detractors I have personally owned some of these small inexpensive guns. Are they as well made as a Colt? No.
Are they capable of saving your life in an armed confrontation? You can bet your life they are, and they have done so on many occasions.

Gun ownership can never and should never be only about the rights of the better off individuals; it is the right of all of us.

The NRA has stated that they will continue to represent all gun owners, regardless of the type and make of gun possessed. As they say in those annoying TV promotions, "Membership is not required."

The right- to- carry in National parks was pushed through Congress in 2009, with a massive backing and lobbying effort from the NRA. Without it there would have just been one more part of the U.S.A. where gun owners could not possess a gun for self-defense.

At the time of writing in 2011, The NRA is actively supporting a reciprocatory concealed- carry bill that would have all CCW states recognize each other's permits. The NRA.ILA is also active in the United Nations where it has become the first nongovernmental organization officially recognized by them.

Castle Doctrine laws have now been adopted in 24 states giving homeowners the right to defend themselves with guns if they suffer home invasion. This was relentlessly pushed through by the NRA. Prior to that, some states required you to flee the home and leave the intruder to it.

Castle Doctrine is named after the British common law presumption that an Englishman's home is his castle and he has a right to defend it. This, of course, no longer applies in the UK.

Ironically, if the laws and rights that the NRA have fought for over its history only applied to NRA members, then there would be 4 million gun owners in the U.S., not 80 million. Of course the NRA is there for all gun owners, not just its members. I am amazed, therefore, that their membership is not at least 10 times higher.

In the coming years, new attacks on our gun rights are probably inevitable. The United Nations is putting together a new treaty widely expected to effectively ban private gun ownership for those that are in member nations.
The Secretary of State has already announced that the United States will sign it.

Unfortunately for the current administration, over 50 Senators signed an open letter to the President in 2011, stating that they would never support any legislation that attempted to restrict Second Amendment rights. (See appendix for copies) Those pesky NRA people were at it again.

The election of President Barak Obama in 2008 caused widespread concern among gun- rights advocates who believed him to be a gun- banner in the mould of his Democratic predecessor, President Clinton. This concern led to an almost panic reaction, and a massive increase in sales of guns and ammunition.

Correspondingly, NRA membership also increased, together with the establishment of other pro- gun groups such as the National Association for Gun Rights, and The Second Amendment Foundation.

These groups, though well- intentioned, do compete for the gun owners' backing, possibly harming the NRA strategy. I was particularly dismayed when, in an effort to raise funds, one of them began attacking the NRA, and urging members to leave. In the words of Nigel Farage, the leader of my former Political party in the UK, *"It was like turkeys collectively voting for Christmas."*

However, the infrastructure of the NRA runs deep. It runs a network of recruiters and has active gun- safety programs for schools, including the 'Eddie the Eagle' program.

This is an initiative that essentially teaches children not to play with guns and to tell teachers or adults immediately if they find one.

This program is naturally (and inexplicably) opposed by the Brady group, giving rise to serious doubts as to their publicized commitment to improve the nation's gun safety.

The NRA also has a recognized certification program for instructors and affiliated clubs throughout the U.S.A. These instructors continue to ensure that safe and responsible gun handling is taught at all levels. In fact, some states, such as Ohio accept NRA basic pistol certification as qualification for Carrying Concealed Deadly Weapon certification.

The NRA Institute for Legislative Action (NRA.ILA) is relentless in opposing anti-gun legislation in the courts and is probably the only gun rights group with the necessary resources to do so.

So! What of the NRA's future? Well, the organization will be as good as its members.

Its leaders would do well to take advice
from the Second Amendment's author,
James Madison. And listen to the people,
not just to it's now 4 million-plus NRA
members.

Its constant lobbying and opposition to anti -
gun legislation culminated in the Heller
decision of 2008 by the U.S. Supreme Court,
which reaffirmed that the right to keep and
bear arms applied to individuals under the
Second Amendment.

However, the NRA does have its critics
among gun- owners. Their concerns need to
be addressed. Accusations that the
organization works too closely with
legislators and they constantly harass
members for more donations, are among the
more frequent complaints. This was often
the reason given for a declining NRA
membership. The events of Sandy Hook and
renewed concern over gun control, have
reversed that decline and this is all to the
good.

Americas' gun- owners need to express their
concerns directly to the NRA leadership,
and that leadership needs to start listening.

A large increase in NRA membership would undoubtedly push back the influence of the gun- control lobby in the United States. Conversely continued infighting and criticism as is rife in the National Association for Gun Rights, will likely lead to a loss of influence and a subsequent advance towards UK style gun control in the nation.

Chapter 4

<u>The UK Debacle</u>

English scholar, Granville Sharpe, who helped bring about the abolition of slavery in England and supported American independence, wrote in 1782 that *"No Englishman can be truly loyal who opposes the principles of English law whereby the people are required to have arms of defense and peace, for mutual as well as private defense."*

In the past, the laws of England always required the people to be armed, and not only armed but, to be expert in arms."

In 1785, William Blizard, chief legal advisor to London's mayor and city council, stated, "The right of his majesty's Protestant subjects, to have arms for their own defense, and to use them for lawful purposes, is most clear and undeniable."

It seems, indeed, to be considered, by the ancient laws of this kingdom, not only as a right, but as a duty.

Unfortunately for the English people, they have been persuaded by their own far-left government and insidious anti-gun activists to allow the English Bill of Rights to be totally trashed. Today, the English do not have the right to keep and bear arms for self-preservation and defense. As a direct result, they live in a crime-ridden society that grows worse with each passing day.

The recent 2000 International Crime Victims Survey, published by the Dutch Ministry of Justice, produced a highly respected and accurate measurement of the percentage of people, by nation, who are victims of violent crimes. It ranked England far ahead of the United States (which ranked 8th), and second only to Australia (where English-style anti-gun laws are also in effect) as the most violent nation. A recently disarmed England now has twice as much violent crime per capita as the United States.

Commenting on the early legal requirement that every American male and every American household be armed, attorney Don B. Kates said that citizens "were not simply *allowed* to keep their own arms, but affirmatively *required* to do so."

He further said that these statutes reflect the classical worldview that "arms possession for protection of self, family and polity was both the hallmark of the individual's freedom and one of the two primary factors in his developing the independent, self-reliant, responsible character which classical political philosophers deemed necessary to the citizenry of a free state."

So, what caused England to go on to enact such Draconian legislation as exists there today? Despite the overwhelming evidence that such laws contribute to, and facilitate, violence, it probably started with the 1937 Firearms Act, which imposed age restrictions on anyone purchasing firearms, and other controls excepting shotguns. In the same year, the Home Secretary instructed that self-defense was no longer a suitable reason for applying for a firearm certificate, and directed police to refuse such applications on the grounds that "firearms cannot be regarded as a suitable means of protection, and may be a source of danger."

Although this instruction should have led to outrage with the clouds of war gathering over Europe, the British had other things on their mind, and the lawmakers moved a step closer to total disarmament.

(Does the political phrase, "Never let a good crisis go to waste" come to mind here?) Anyway let us go back to a time that common sense ruled in England, before the dark times, Before the Empire (*with apologies to George Lucas*)

TEENAGE MEMORIES

Like most of us who are now gun- owners, I recall my first *'real gun'*.

I was a young teenager who had bought and used an air rifle in the woods around my home, deep in the Cotswold Hills of Gloucestershire in Central England.

There was no shortage of older boys and men in the village, who were willing to show me how to hold the gun and shoot it. In those halcyon days of the 50s and 60s, WW2 vets, like their American counterparts, tried to temper their children's natural interest in guns, with the need to teach responsibility and safe handling.

My father was such a man. Dad always was reluctant to encourage my shooting. This may have been a throwback from his military service.

Though my father never saw active service in WW2, he was well aware of the sacrifice and inglorious carnage that the conflict had wrought.

Around this time, I had acquired a smooth bore 9mm garden gun from a friend, for a few shillings. This was frankly, a dangerous weapon. A single shot, bolt- action carbine with a barrel length of 19 inches. The bolt was loose, and often flew open when fired.

The little 9mm silver metal cartridge cases were packed with shot, and it had an effective range of about 20 feet. My targets were usually Rats small birds, and the occasional tin can.

At this time, all firearms were subject to the Firearms Act 1937, and this defined shotguns with a barrel length of more than 20 inches. If they were less than that, they were subject to the more rigorous firearm certificate legislation.

I was, of course unaware of this until I took the gun to my local gun shop to get the bolt fixed and they told me it was illegal to possess it. And anyway, repairs would be difficult.

Being a strong- headed (Or should that be pig -headed) teenager, I went to the local police station to check on this, and seek a second opinion. The desk sergeant checked the gun over and after some suspicious questioning, became helpful, and suggested I surrender the gun back to the same (and only) gun store for disposal, and in future - buy one from a more reputable source.

He recommended I buy a. 410 from the same gun shop. So, I duly returned, and after some negotiation, I settled on a. 410 break action shotgun. This was a little expensive for my budget, but in the eyes of a youngster, brought up on a diet of American westerns, it had one great feature: On the receiver was stamped, "Winchester Repeating Arms Co. Hartford, Connecticut."

That did it for me; I felt like John Wayne and Matt Dillon rolled into one. With that trusty 410, I learned to shoot properly, under the patient tutelage of the local gamekeeper on the estate where my father worked.
He taught me to identify targets, shoot on the wing, and how to mount, shoot, and care for my gun.

It started me off on a life of shooting and a love of firearms that has brought me from the green hills of the English Cotswold's to a rural farm in Kentucky.
It also brought me from a time when common sense and a responsible attitude to firearms was commonplace, to a time of fear, misinformation, and Draconian restrictions on gun ownership that have pushed violent crime in my home country to frightening levels.

I am convinced that any 17-year-old teenager walking into a police station in 2011 England for advice on a gun would not be treated anything remotely close to how I was received. More likely they would trigger panic, an armed response, arrest, and imprisonment.

....

So, how, and why, did England fall so far, and more importantly, can it happen here in the U.S.A.?

Politics has always clouded the issues. The next chapter in the British Governments relentless drive to ban guns continued with a well-organized anti- gun lobby that successfully appealed to the understandable horror of two shooting incidents.

The first of these was an incident in the market town of Hungerford in Berkshire on August 19th 1987.

Twenty seven year old Michael Ryan walked through the streets of that sleepy town. He was armed with two semi- automatic rifles and a handgun, and he used them to devastating effect, killing 16 people, one of whom was his own mother. Ryan later shot himself, when surrounded by police. The gun- control advocates mounted a media blitz on the evils of gun ownership, and the British people demanded something be done.

Politicians as usual, rose to the challenge. They passed the Firearms (amendment) Act, 1988.

This act banned the ownership of semi automatic rifles and placed severe restrictions on shotgun ownership.

The Hungerford massacre was used as the reason for these measures. Even though Ryan did not use one, shotgun controls were imposed.

At this time firearms restrictions in the UK were already pretty stringent. In fact, by American standards, they were deemed Draconian.
Nor were Britain's gun owners in a position to effectively fight the ban.

At the, time of the shootings there were a number of pro gun groups in the UK. Among them, were the National Rifle Association (no connection with the American NRA), The Shooters Rights Association, and the Sportsman's Association.

These Groups collectively had little interaction, and infighting among them quickly destroyed any likelihood of them mounting a serious challenge to the growing influence of the gun- control lobby.

Prior to the ban, the law regarding firearms in the UK was governed by the Firearms Act 1968.

This required that any citizen wishing to own a gun first apply to his local police force for an application for the grant of a firearm certificate. This form required full details of the applicant, the type, and number of firearms requested, and the amount of ammunition desired to be held.

The application also demanded the reason for the request. The form made it clear that personal defense was not considered a valid reason. In fact, the allowable reasons were pretty narrow, but included hunting and target shooting. If target shooting was chosen, membership of a shooting club was mandatory and the application had to be countersigned by the club secretary who normally required 6 months of membership before signing.

Once submitted with the appropriate fee, a police officer was tasked with visiting the applicant, checking the details and, in particular, the security measures in place to secure the weapon.

After the interview, the officer would submit a report with his recommendations as to the grant or otherwise of the required certificate.

92

If granted, the certificate was valid for 3 years, and its production was required to purchase a gun and to purchase ammunition.

The certificate also gave the maximum amount of ammunition that could be purchased and possessed at any one time.

As a serving officer with Britain's Hampshire Constabulary, at this time, I was often given the task of doing these investigations. My senior officers knew of my interest in firearms. The fact that I was an instructor and secretary of the police divisional pistol club made me suitable in their eyes to carry out this task.

Unfortunately, some of my colleagues did not have my insight, and I recall one morning being approached by a young officer who was considering rejecting an application he was handling. He came to me because the applicant, a local publican, (owner, and licensee of a public bar) knew me, and during his interview, had mentioned this fact.

I enquired as to his concerns and his reply surprised me.

He said he felt the applicant was a danger to himself and the public, as he made his own ammunition, using a press, and fired cases that he reloaded.

This may astonish American gun owners, but it must be stated that at this time, the investigating officer was not required to have any knowledge of firearms, or their use.

My colleague's concern was understandable, and I was happy to reassure him.

Following the introduction of the 1988 Act, the gun- control lobby was given new life and continued their attacks on the private ownership of guns. They had to wait another eight years before they got their chance to achieve the total ban.

On March 13th, 1996, shopkeeper and former scout leader, Thomas Hamilton walked to the Primary (first grade) school in the sleepy Scottish town of Dunblane.

Hamilton was an unstable man who had been granted a certificate for firearms, largely because of his stated desire to use them in the training of scouting troops under his stewardship.

However, allegations about his unhealthy interest in young boys had led to his firing as, a leader from three Stirlingshire scout troops and suspension from the national Scouting Association.

Surprisingly, such conduct had not reached the ears of the local police, who cheerfully renewed his certificate for the guns he later used.

Hamilton became very bitter, and his resentment towards the Police and residents of Dunblane continued to grow. It would soon explode into an orgy of unbelievable horror. As he entered the school, Hamilton wore a baseball cap and ear protection. He carried two 9mm Browning semi- automatic pistols and two Smith and Wesson .357 magnum revolvers, together with 743 rounds of ammunition.

His destination was the school gymnasium where Primary One, a class of five and six--year olds was assembled with their teacher.

Without warning, Hamilton opened fire. Fifteen children died, together with their class teacher, Gwen Mayor, who was killed while heroically trying to protect the children.

Hamilton then left the gymnasium through the emergency exit, entering the playground outside, and then began shooting into a mobile classroom, reloading as he went. A teacher in the mobile classroom had heard the shooting and realized that something was seriously wrong, and told the terrified children to hide under the tables.

Most of the bullets became embedded in books and equipment, though one passed through a chair which, seconds before, had been used by one of the children.

He also fired at a group of children walking in a corridor, injuring one teacher. Hamilton then returned into the gym, and fired one final shot this one upwards into his mouth, killing him instantly.

Aside from the dead, a further eleven children and three adults were rushed to the hospital as soon as the emergency services arrived. One child, Mhairi Isabel MacBeath, was pronounced dead on arrival at the hospital.

The reaction to the massacre was immediate, and was flashed around the world.

In the UK, a new anti- gun body emerged, The Gun Control Network. It was formed with backing from media and notably the Sunday Mail who launched a massive petition.

(The Gun Control Network can be accurately described as the UK equivalent of the Brady Group in the US). One newspaper even stated boldly that Hamilton had worn ear protectors to avoid hearing the screams of his young victims. News anchors around the country joined in the clamor, and all appeals for restraint and a proper investigation were drowned out by the demands for all guns to be outlawed.

With mounting criticism of the government underway the Prime Minister, John Major, was forced to act and his government instigated an immediate ban on private ownership of all centre fire handguns, excepting. 22 target pistols primarily used for target shooting. They also appointed a parliamentary commission to investigate the incident and make recommendations. Although the commission concluded a total ban on all handguns would not work, would be a panic reaction, and would do little to stop a repeat of the Dunblane incident, the Gun Control Network smelled victory.

They heavily backed the Labour Party in the General Election of 1997 who promised to get rid of guns once and for all. The subsequent election of the Labour Party and the new Prime Minister Tony Blair, gave them what they had worked for, The Firearms Amendment) (No 2) Act 1997.

This act imposed a total ban on all handguns including. 22 rim-fire weapons all of which had to be surrendered without compensation within the grace period, following which, possession of a modern handgun would be punishable by five years imprisonment on first conviction.

So what was the outcome? The 1997 law that Britain passed requiring civilians to surrender almost all privately- owned handguns to the police resulted in more than 162,000 handguns and 1.5 million pounds of ammunition being "compulsorily surrendered" by February 1998.

The Home Office used the data from records on firearms certificates to enable them to swiftly check on the legal guns in circulation. This resulted in tracing all but about eight of all legally- owned handguns in England, Scotland, and Wales.

In effect, the certificates were used as a gun-registration database. This is something that we need to remember when the notion of gun registration is raised in the future here.

However, contrary to general belief, the United Kingdom does not have a total handgun Ban. The six counties that make up the province of Northern Ireland retained a right to keep their arms under the Firearms Certificate procedure when the 1997 ban came into effect.

The reason is unclear, but there is still a high security risk in Northern Ireland, which has been involved in their own war on terror. Sectarian murders and shootings have not ended with the much heralded one- sided peace agreement. The IRA terror group has not disbanded nor changed their stated aims of a United Ireland, regardless of the wishes of the province who have constantly voted to remain part of the United Kingdom. It is wildly believed that the stockpile of weapons held by them are fully available and have been updated.

The law enforcement personnel, Judiciary, and others involved in the fight against the IRA before the peace agreement, along with former military personnel, are still seen as legitimate targets to the terrorists who have succeeded in negotiating the release of all convicted IRA members from Northern Ireland jails.

Clearly these people are at risk and the chief constable is still able to issue certificates for firearms for personal defense purposes. Before issue, the chief constable must be satisfied that the applicant:

1. 　　　Is not prohibited by law from possessing a firearm, is not of intemperate habits or unsound mind, and is not, for any reason, unfit to be entrusted with a firearm.
2. 　　　Has good reason for purchasing, acquiring, or having in their possession the firearm or ammunition in respect of which the application is made.
3. 　　　Can be permitted to have that firearm or ammunition in their possession without danger to public safety or to the peace.

The criteria are the same as were in place in the rest of the UK before the gun ban. Strict, but at least the police do allow citizens there, to own firearms.

The estimated total number of guns held by civilians in Northern Ireland is 380,000 The rate of private gun ownership in Northern Ireland is 21.9 firearms per 100 people. And yes, you've guessed it: gun crime is on the decline there, compared to the rest of the UK.

On the night of 20 August 1999, two burglars, Brendon Fearon, 29, and Fred Barras, 16 broke into an isolated farmhouse in Emneth, in Hungate Norfolk, East Anglia. While the two entered the House, a third man Darren Bark, 33, waited outside in a getaway car.

Tony Martin had inherited the house from his uncle at age 35 and lived alone, the house was known locally as Bleak House. This fact was known as was the fact that the police response time was up to an hour ,which made the farmer a target for local criminals who had already hit the farmhouse ten times, stealing furniture an antique clock and silverware, with a total value of £6,000 (approx $10,000). Martin had also complained about police inaction over the burglaries.

The police reports from the time do state that multiple items and furniture were stolen such as the dinnerware and grandfather clock. Martin had reported the matter each time but without result, other than the police filling out the standard report.

It is fair to say that by the night of August 20th, Martin had reached the end of his patience. As the two burglars entered his house, Martin opened fire with his Winchester pump- action 12 gauge. Fearon was hit in the leg and Barras in the back. Barras escaped through the window, but died at the scene.

This time the Police did take action. They arrested Martin for murder and Fearon and Bark for conspiracy to burgle. Martin's plea of self- defense was rejected by the police without consideration. The dead Youth was hardly an innocent victim. Although only sixteen yrs old he already had a long police record having been arrested 29 times, had served two months for assaulting a police officer, and for theft and being drunk and disorderly. On the night he died Barras was awaiting trial after being charged with the theft of garden furniture, and was out on bail.

At his trial Martin, stated he had shot downwards towards the intruders, and had not intended to kill them.

On 10, January 2000, Fearon and Bark, (who had acted as the getaway driver), both from Newark-on-Trent, Nottinghamshire, admitted to conspiring to burgle Martin's farmhouse. Fearon was sentenced to three years in prison and Bark to thirty months (with an additional 12 months arising from previous offences). Fearon was released on 10, August 2001.

English law permits one person to kill another in self- defense only if the person defending him- or herself uses no more than "reasonable force"; it is the responsibility of the jury to determine whether or not an unreasonable amount of force was used. However, the law is also clear that any force used cannot be in excess of the force used by the attacker. Unlike in the U.S.A., self, defense was not considered a reason to employ deadly force.

I myself witnessed this in the early 80s while attending a murder trial at Winchester Crown Court.

In summing up the judge was asked to explain the law of reasonable force. He did so by offering the following example.

A victim may only use force equal to that of the attacker. If a man attacks you with a knife, you could not for example pull out a gun and shoot him, which would be totally out of proportion to the force used.

With such laws, Tony Martins fate was sealed.

The case aroused considerable anger in the UK, and most of the media sided with Martin. At the trial, the jury was told that they had the option of returning a verdict of manslaughter, rather than murder, but only if they thought that Martin "did not intend to kill or cause serious bodily harm." This left them no room to bring in a not- guilty verdict. The jurors found Martin guilty of murder by a 10 to 2 majority.

He was sentenced to life in prison, the mandatory sentence for murder, as England has no death penalty.

Barras's family then sued Martin for damages, unfortunately this is a trend often seen on this side of the Atlantic.

This prompted Martin's solicitor, Nick Makin, to make the following statement.

"It is appalling that the family of someone who has a criminal record for burglary and assault should attempt to claim any damages of criminal injury when he was shot while burgling the dwelling of an innocent person...

It is also appalling that they may get legal aid while his victim is in prison and patently unable to work and equally cannot get legal aid... There is something wrong and perverse with our legal system that it permits this."

This is a sentiment with which most citizens in the U.S.A. would agree.

An appeal was filed on behalf of Martin and was considered in October 2001 by three senior judges headed by Lord Woolf. Submissions by the defense that Martin had fired in his own defense were rejected by the appeal court in view of the Home Office direction that firearms cannot be considered a suitable means of defense; this was hardly surprising.

Anticipating this, the defense also submitted evidence that Martin suffered from paranoid personality disorder, specifically directed at anyone intruding into his home. (Who wouldn't?)

This submission was accepted by the Court of Appeal, and on the grounds of diminished responsibility.

Martin's murder conviction was replaced by manslaughter, carrying a five-year sentence, and his ten-year sentence for wounding Fearon was reduced to three years.

These sentences were to run concurrently.

Martin was imprisoned at Highpoint Prison, Suffolk. When he became eligible for parole and early release in January 2003, the parole board rejected his application without stating a reason. The chairman of the parole board, Sir David Hatch, in an interview with The Times newspaper described Martin as "a very dangerous man" who may still believe, his action had been right.

This statement from a leading lawmaker shows just how out- of- touch the British Government was, with the general public who overwhelmingly supported the luckless farmer.

Martin challenged the decision in the High Court, where the parole board's decision was upheld. Probation officers on Martin's cases said there was an "unacceptable risk" that Martin might again react with excessive force if other would-be burglars intruded on his Norfolk farm.

The unbelievable attitude of these so- called civil servants shows only to clearly the way the whole British judicial system has, fallen under the gun control lobby propaganda machine.

On 28 July 2003, Martin was released after serving three years of his five -year sentence, the maximum period for which he could be held following good behavior.

During 2003, Fearon applied for, and received, an estimated £5,000 of legal aid allowing him to sue Martin for loss of earnings due to the injuries he had sustained.

However, the merits of the case were thrown into doubt when photographs were published in The Sun newspaper (which had championed Martins cause) showing him "cycling and climbing with little apparent difficulty", While the case was pending suggesting that Fearon's injuries were not as serious as had been claimed.

Fearon was recalled to jail after being charged with the theft of a vehicle while on probation on a conviction for dealing heroin. His case was falling apart and Fearon agreed to drop it if Martin agreed to drop a counter-claim.

Tens of thousands of pounds of public money had been spent on the case. But it did highlight the public interest, and that of the media. The BBC reported in 2003 that Fearon's supporters put a bounty on Martin's head, of several tens of thousands of pounds. In the same year, The Guardian newspaper reported that a cousin of Barras had said that a £60,000 bounty had been put on Martin's head.

In October 2003, The Daily Mirror newspaper paid Martin £125,000 for an exclusive interview on his release from prison.

After investigation, the Press Complaints Commission ruled that the payment was justified and in the public interest because Martin "had a unique insight into an issue of great public concern."

Since his release, Tony Martin has become a hero to the gun- rights lobby in the UK and has become an active political speaker appearing on the platform of the United Kingdom Independence Party in the UK as well as endorsing more extreme right- wing parties such as the British National Party (BNP), and The National Front.

The case of Tony Martin did much to highlight the injustice felt in Britain where the people have at last began to question much of Tony Blair's socialist agenda.

In the General Election of 2010, the Labor Party was defeated and David Cameron's incoming conservative coalition started to reverse the anti-self-defense laws of the previous government. They also have announced plans to re-introduce limited target shooting for Olympic- type events.

The UK currently has the most restrictive gun- ownership laws in Europe and of course one of the highest gun- crime rates. The right of self-defense in the UK is also virtually non- existent. This has of course had a number of effects.

The UK Olympic shooting teams have been prevented from owning or training in the UK, effectively eliminating any chance of serious competitiveness.

The ban, of course has had no effect on the reduction of crime. In fact, statistics released from the UK Home Office show the opposite is true. So! The gun- control lobby had won in the UK. Now they looked west, towards the United States.

The right to defend one's home and one's person when attacked has been guaranteed through the ages by common law."

- Martin Luther King

Chapter 5

<u>The State of Britain, Post Gun- Ban</u>

The total ban on all modern handguns in 1988, following the Dunblane massacre in Scotland, was, if you believed the British Government, going to herald in a safer society. Well, in the years since, what has actually happened?

Statistics, put out by the Government, The Gun Control Network and other sources were completely at odds with each other, both in the UK and elsewhere. So, to put things into perspective let us concentrate on gun violence, which is the use of firearms by criminals.

A Home Office study published in 2007 reported that gun crime in England & Wales remained a relatively rare event. Firearms (including air guns) were used in 21,521-recorded crimes. It said that injury caused during a firearm offence was rare, with fewer than 3% resulting in a serious or fatal injury.

The number of homicides per year committed with firearms had remained between a range of 49 and 97 in the eight years prior to 2006. There were two fatal shootings of police officers in England and Wales in this period, and 107 non-fatal shootings, an average of 9.7 per year over the same period.

Comparisons between the U.S.A. and the UK, of course have to take into account the population and size of each country. Most statisticians (Gun Control Network excepted) use the ratio of 1 to 100,000 per population, so let us begin there.

In 2005-6 the police in England and Wales reported fifty gun homicides, a rate of 0.1 illegal gun deaths per 100,000 of population. Only 6.6% of homicides involved the use of a firearm. By way of international comparison, in 2004, the police in the United States reported 9,326 gun homicides.

The overall homicide rates per 100,000 (regardless of weapon type) reported by the United Nations for 1999 were 4.55 for the U.S. and 1.45 in England and Wales. It is not known on what basis these figures were compiled.

The homicide rate in England and Wales at the end of the 1990s was below the EU average, but the rates in Northern Ireland and Scotland were above the EU average.

While the number of crimes involving firearms in England and Wales increased from 13,874 in 1998-99 to 24,070 in 2002/03, they remained relatively static at 24,094 in 2003-04 and have since fallen to 21,521 in 2005-06. The latter includes 3,275 crimes involving imitation firearms and 10,437 involving air weapons, compared to 566 and 8,665 respectively in 1998-99.

Of course, in the UK only those "firearms" positively identified as being imitations or air weapons, for example, by being recovered by the police at the scene or by being actually discharged, are classed as firearms offences as such, so the actual numbers are likely to be significantly higher.

This manipulation in reporting firearms figures is common with governments who desire to produce data that support their contentions. (The Brady group is an absolute master at this.)

In 2005-06, 8,978 of the total of 21,521 firearms crimes (42%) were for criminal damage. The UK Home Office tends to change the numbers to suit the mood. For example, prior to the gun- ban, they needed to boost gun- crime figures, so they included cases of poaching, certificate mistakes, and juveniles misusing air or BB guns, e.g. breaking windows. Once the gun- ban was in force, these statistics needed reductions, so only criminals using real firearms in crimes were included.

Wow! So they make magical reduction in the statics to keep a nervous population happy.

I personally witnessed this during a police amnesty for guns in Hampshire. The public were asked to surrender guns they held, under an assurance that there would be no repercussions.

(Ironically, if a member of the public brought a gun into the police Station outside this amnesty they would be liable to arrest, and several were.)

The number of guns handed in during the four-week amnesty was approximately 2,400.

This was In Southern England in the county of Hampshire where I was a serving officer. This was good news for the police and the government. The police proudly displayed the haul at its headquarters in Winchester, for the media.

Unfortunately, a young reporter who was sharper than most, asked how many of the guns were actually illegal weapons, rifles, revolvers and such, that would normally have been subject to firearm certificates. When the police, reluctantly gave the answer the figure tanked dramatically. The result then, was that approximately ninety were actually illegal guns. When toy guns, cigarette lighters, BB guns, Air guns and replica and dummy guns were taken out of the equation, a truer picture emerged. (*Do I hear another drat and double drat here*)

I am grateful for that unnamed reporter for exposing this. My position as a police officer made it impossible for me to object, officially. And in any case, knowing my view on the whole charade, my senior officers made sure I was not part of the amnesty operation.

Now, let me be clear. I have no problem with amnesties that remove guns from people who no longer want them and wish to ensure that they are kept out of the wrong hands. My beef is when such an operation is hijacked for political ends.

This sleight of hand is not confined to Great Britain. The gun control lobby over here has made it into a real art form.

Compared with the United States of America, the United Kingdom has, according to official sources, a slightly higher total crime rate per capita of approximately 85 per 1000 people, while in the U.S.A. it is at approximately 80.

Since 1998, the number of people injured by firearms in England and Wales increased by 110%, from 2,378 in 1998-99 to 5,001 in 2005/06.

Most of the rise was in the category of slight injuries from non-air weapons. 'Slight' in this context means an injury that was not classified as 'serious' (i.e., did not require detention in the hospital, did not involve fractures, concussion, severe general shock, penetration by a bullet or multiple shot wounds).

This definition includes the use of firearms as a threat only. In 2005-06, 87% of such injuries were defined as "slight."

In 2007, the British government was accused by Shadow Home Secretary David Davis (British Conservative Party) of making "inaccurate and misleading" statements claiming that gun- crime was falling, after official figures showed that gun-related killings and injuries recorded by police had risen more than fourfold since 1998, mainly due to a rise in non-fatal injuries. Mr. Davis was correct in his assessment. As usual, this fact was buried by the UK Media.

Justice Minister, Mr. Jack Straw told the BBC, "We are concerned that within the overall record, which is a good one, of crime going down in the last 10-11 years, the number of gun-related incidents has gone up. But it has now started to fall." Despite his assurances gun related incidents have continued to rise.

In 2008 the liberal British newspaper *The Independent* reported that there were 42 gun-related deaths in Great Britain, a twenty -year low.

However, in late 2009 the more conservative *Daily Telegraph* reported that gun crime had doubled in the last 10 years, with an increase in both firearms offences and deaths. A government spokesman sheepishly admitted this was correct, saying that this increase was a result of a change in reporting practices in 2001. He added that gun crime had actually fallen since 2005.

So! The conclusion appears to be that, if you are careful in what incidents you include, and how you classify a gun crime, and then you can make the figures look pretty good. But all this is of little comfort to the citizen who has no recourse when attacked or threatened in their home or while going about their daily lives. And remember, gun crime, it was promised, would not be a problem once guns were outlawed.

So how do these statistics relate to real life in the post gun ban UK?

Let's examine more closely some of the incidents in Tony Blair's Utopian gun free Britain since the Ban came into force.

Over the course of a few days in the summer of 2001, gun-toting men burst into an English court and freed two defendants.

A shooting outside a London nightclub left five women and three men wounded. Two men were machine-gunned to death in a residential neighborhood of north London. And on New Year's Day 2002 a nineteen-year-old girl walking on a main street in east London, was shot in the head by a thief who wanted her mobile phone.

London police stated at the time that they were looking to see if the New York City police and its then- Mayor Rudi Giuliani could offer any advice. That announcement went down like a lead balloon with the Gun-Control Network.

Among all this, three incidents do stand out. And we will examine each of them in more detail.

January 2nd 2003: Birmingham, England

The New Year's Eve night out turned deadly for partygoers Letisha and Charlene aged 17 and 18 respectively. Both girls died in a hail of sub- machine gun fire, the result of a violent feud between two drug gangs, The Johnson Crew and the Burger Bar Boys.

The assailants had used a Mac-10 sub-machine gun, often nicknamed the 'spray and pray' because its fierce recoil makes it almost impossible to aim accurately. To repeat, this was Birmingham England, 2003, in Blair's Gun Free Britain, not Chicago, Illinois, 1926.

Saturday, 19 November 2005 Bradford England

Two female officers both unarmed and with less than two year's experience of policing, had been called to a shop in the city centre in response to an alarm. This is a common occurrence during opening hours, when staff often forget to deactivate alarms while opening secure doors and such, and one of which as a Police Officer, I was very familiar with.

As the officers arrived at the travel agency, up to three men ran from the premises. One shot was fired initially, and was the fatal shot. More shots were fired shortly afterwards.

Pc Beshenivsky, a 38-year-old mother, was killed as she arrived at the scene on the day of her youngest daughter's fourth birthday. Her colleague Pc Teresa Milburn was also shot and paralyzed as the robbers escaped with little more than £5,000., ($7,500).

June 3rd, 2010:

Derek Bird

Despite the total gun ban on handguns in the United Kingdom, and despite what figures the government there continue to churn out. Mass shootings still do occur. Such an incident was committed in June 2nd 2010 in the north of England. The perpetrator Derek Bird aged 52, a self-employed taxi driver who legally owned a rifle and a shotgun. The incident began when Bird, , shot dead his twin brother, David Bird, in Lamplugh, He then drove to the nearby town of Frizington and shot dead the family solicitor, Kevin Commons. At 10:20 am, the police were telephoned. By then Bird had driven on to Whitehaven. At 10:33, He shot dead a taxi driver close to the taxi rank in Whitehaven. It emerged that the suspect, later identified as Bird's victim was known to him, and that he had also shot several others.

Soon after this, residents in the towns of Whitehaven, Egremont, and Seascale were urged by the police to stay indoors after the shots were heard and there were further shooting incidents. As Police Officers are not routinely armed in the UK, there was no opposition. Bird then drove through several local towns firing apparently at random. In Egremont, Bird killed a further two people on the streets. The couple was both shot dead in the village of and a mole-catcher in working in a field in was also shot dead by the deranged killer. A former semi-professional rugby league player, Garry Purdham, was shot dead outside the Red Admiral Hotel at Boonwood, near Gosforth. Bird also killed three people in Seascale: two pedestrians and a man driving a car. The motorist died, although it was not clear at first whether he died from gunshot wounds or the resultant car crash.[

Police announced they were searching for the driver of a dark grey Citroën Xsara, driven by the suspect who they identified as Derek. Shortly afterwards Bird abandoned his car in the village of Boot and continued to evade the police on foot. Armed police units were moved into the area, and a search made. At 14:00, they came upon Birds in a wooded area, along with a rifle.

Later that evening, a police press conference in Whitehaven announced that 12 people had been killed, that a further 11 people were injured, and that the suspect had killed himself. They also confirmed that two weapons (a double barreled shotgun and a. 22 caliber rifle with a telescopic sight and silencer on, had been used by the suspect in the attacks and that thirty different crime scenes were being investigated. Slowly the police put together all the incidents. It was found that the shootings had taken place along a 15-mile (24 km) stretch of the Cumbrian coastline.[Bird had been a licensed firearms holder and the incident inevitably sparked debate about further gun control measures. As usual this took precedence over the mindset of the perpetrator.

So who was this mad gunman who treated the picturesque area of Cumbria as his own personal shooting gallery, with live targets?

Derrick Bird, was indeed a licensed gun owner, both his shotgun and rifle were permitted under the UK certification system. His Shotgun certificate had been issued in 1974 and had been renewed every 5 years. His Firearm certificate was issued in 2007.

He was a quite man who worked as a self-employed taxi driver in Whitehaven. There are unconfirmed reports that he had previously sought help from a local hospital due to his fragile mental state. Bird had held a shotgun certificate since 1974 and had renewed it a number of times, most recently in 2005, and had held a firearms certificate for a rifle from 2007 onwards. He was being investigated by HM Revenue and Customs (IRS).

The body of Bird was formally identified at and he was cremated at a private service on 18 June 2010.

A fellow taxi driver, who described himself as one of Bird's best friends, and was shot in the hand, has claimed that Bird had a relationship with a Thai girl he met on holiday in Pattaya, Thailand. It has been further claimed by another friend of Bird that he had sent the sum of one thousands pounds (approximately $1700.00) to the girl, who subsequently ended their relationship via a text message; Friends of his had told him bluntly he had been "made a fool out of."

There was further speculation that Bird had been involved with a family dispute over his father's will. Evidence of this is that Bird had targeted his twin, David, and the family's solicitor, Kevin Commons, in his attacks, killing both. Police investigating the killings have also found that Bird was the subject of an ongoing tax investigation by HM revenue and Customs for tax evasion. This suggests that he could have been under pressure by the threat of possible future prosecution and punishment at the time of the killings, suggesting a possible cause of his actions. According to Mark Cooper, a fellow taxi driver who had known him for 15 years, Bird had accumulated £60,000 in a secret bank account and was worried he would be sent to prison for hiding the cash from HM Revenue & Customs. There is no doubt that Bird had a fragile mental state, though suggestions that he may have sought medical assistance have not been confirmed.

There are of course many other examples I could quote. Arguments will of course continue on both sides as to what these incidents mean. However two facts do stand out. Firstly the ban on handguns has not stopped the criminal use of handguns in the UK. It is an unmitigated disaster.

Secondly the citizens of the UK were clearly duped by the Gun Control Network, and the government into rushing to support a knee-jerk reaction to a shooting, without first considering any consequences.

Gun crime is just a part of Britain's increasingly lawless environment. From 1991 to 1995, crimes against the individual person in England's inner cities increased by ninety one percent. And in the four years from 1997 to 2001, the rate of violent crime in general has more than doubled.

Your chances of being mugged in London are now six times greater than in New York City.

England's rates of assault, robbery, and burglary are far higher than America's and 53 percent of English burglaries occur while the occupants are at home, compared with 13 percent in the U.S., where burglars admit to fearing armed homeowners more than they fear the police.

In a United Nations study of crime published in July 2010, of eighteen developed nations, England and Wales led the Western world's crime league with nearly 55 crimes per 100 people.

Of course, Britain does have other problems as well. Years of socialist government following the gun- ban led to a re-defining of self- defense law, putting anyone injuring an intruder or attacker, while trying to defend themselves faced certain arrest, and probable jail time.

The supremacy of E.U. law over British law also meant that free passage of persons between member states could not be impeded. This led to a massive influx of illegal guns flooding the black market and quickly ending up on the streets of Britain, in the hands of various drug gangs. All of this was totally ignored by the Home Office (The equivalent of the Department. of Justice in U.S.).

The Blair government insisted that it was in control and outbreaks of gun violence were blamed on something the prime minister called 'Gun Culture.'

In turn, this was used to justify more and more ridiculous legal actions to turn the tide. Replica guns were banned to all but high-profile reenactment groups, and even they had to be approved by the Home Office and carry high public liability insurance.

Police quickly moved against country and
western clubs and smaller living history
organizations. Deactivated weapons were
also brought under strict police control and
require deactivation by an approved
Government proof house at a cost of around
$180.00. These restrictions were imposed in
despite an assurance from the government
while passing the 1989 Act that they had no
intention of doing so. A country music event
at Brean, in Somerset also was targeted
when U.S. Civil war re-enactors were
forbidden to carry unsheathed sabers during
parades.

In early June 2008, an incident occurred at
Britain's Heathrow Airport which illustrated
how things had deteriorated.

Thirty-year-old Brad Jayakody was shocked
when he was told by airport security to
change his shirt if he wanted to catch his
flight from Terminal 5. Jayakody, who,
along with four colleagues, was on a British
Airways trip to Dusseldorf, Germany, was
wearing a white T-shirt with a line drawing
graphic of a Transformer cartoon character
on the front.

The Transformer robot held a fantasy ray
gun.

Staggered, Jayakody asked to see the security chief. He probably thought the security guard's boss would 'see sense' but incredibly the supervisor backed up the decision and threatened Jayakody with arrest.

Australian- born Brad is quoted as saying, "My mate set off the alarms and was searched. But, then the guy told me to stop, and said, "You cannot get on the plane, because there is a gun on your T-shirt." (You just could not make this stuff up, could you?)

Following my departure from the Police Force and for a few months prior to emigrating to the U.S., I worked for a security company in Southampton Docks. (A similar job to the TSA agents in the U.S.) This job involved me screening cruise liner passengers, both by x-ray and searching. The standing orders were that anything that even looked like a weapon was banned and had to be confiscated.

Belt buckles that depicted a gun in relief, and kids' plastic ray guns were quickly seized as being a potential security risk.

One American lady had purchased a plastic sword for her son, and the toy was in her luggage. It had triggered my suspicion when it lit up the x-ray as possibly metallic. The Rapsicon x-ray machine was able to determine organic, non-organic, liquid, and metallic objects, by color and density.

When examined, it was obvious that the sword was made of harmless plastic and that the alarm had been triggered by the toy's silver- metallic paint. I therefore requested that the lady be allowed to keep the sword. To my astonishment the request was refused, the supervisor insisting that even metal paint could pose a security risk.

Thankfully I was able to leave that company shortly afterwards to escape the madness and relocate to the U.S.A.

In October 2008, I left the chaos of Britain to fly to Alaska and start a new life with my wife, Eva. But I also made the mistake of using London's Heathrow Airport.

In my check- in luggage, I had a case containing two blank- firing prop guns, peacemaker revolvers.

Since I had been working in Southampton screening trans-Atlantic passengers departing and arriving on the Ocean Liners, I was aware that these guns would show up as potential weapons on x- rays and may generate problems.

I had resisted multiple advices to surrender the guns to the Police for destruction as these guns had been used by me over the previous twenty-five years in western themed pageants, and were of great sentimental value.

They were fitted with solid metal barrels and were therefore incapable of firing live ammunition. Having called the airline ahead of time and explaining that I was taking these guns to my new home in Alaska, I asked them what I needed to do to ensure a trouble free exit. I was told to declare them at check- in and they would inform Customs who would check them before clearing them to be taken out of the country.

Despite this assurance, I arrived an hour early, as I expected hassle and was not disappointed. A Customs official first suggested I take the guns out in the concourse, so he could look at them.

I pointed out that taking out two revolvers in a crowded airport concourse post- 9/11 may not be the smartest thing to do. I suggested instead that we go to his office and allow him to examine the guns in private. After some thought, he agreed. In his office I stripped the guns to show him that there was no chamber or bore and the barrels were solid.

After looking at them he announced, as he was not an expert in guns, and he could not give me clearance or take my word for it that the guns could not fire. However to assist, he would consult the chief of the airport Tactical Firearms Unit (U.K. S.W.A.T.) to seek advice. I'm not sure how he though a gun with a solid barrel, would be able to fire a bullet, but I bit my tongue.

On his return with conformation from the TFU inspector that the guns were harmless more arguments followed, as he now insisted I should have a police firearms certificate even if the guns didn't work.

I again pointed out that as, they were not guns, and the police would not issue a certificate. I finally got him to reluctantly give me a clearance slip and after showing him how to fill it out, I caught my flight.

Needless to say, once I landed in the U.S.A. I had no further problems. The 'guns' made it to my new home in Alaska and currently they adorn my fireplace in Kentucky. They are a constant reminder of the madness of England's gun laws.

I am sure the reader may find these two stories amusing, if not frustrating, but after my initial anger I was left with a sense of sadness that a former great nation had been reduced to the laughing stock of Europe.

Not only has gun- control in the U.K. totally failed, it has actually made the situation far worse. In the U.S.A., I am now a Concealed Carry Permit holder and have no fear going about my daily business secure in the knowledge I am able to defend myself. To me, the land of the Free is exactly that.

By contrast, when on trips back to the UK I am now in real fear of having to walk around unarmed with no right to defend myself, or my wife, in a society more violent than the U.S.A. I have little optimism that anything will change there in the near future.

The police there of course are not to blame. As here, in the U.S. they do not make the law; they merely have to enforce it regardless of how irrational that law may be.

No! In my opinion, the blame lies with the gun-control network and liberal politicians whose political agenda pushed through ill thought out and dangerous legislation that has cost countless lives. The blood is squarely and unequivocally on their hands.

There have however been some signs that the UK's attitude on self-defense has been softening lately. Take the case of Andy and Tracey Ferrie, who lived in an isolated farm nr Melton Mowbery in Leicestershire. They were arrested in the early hours of Sunday 2nd September 2012, after Andrew opened fire with his shotgun at two burglars who had broken in to their house during the night. They were held on suspicion of causing grievous bodily harm and spent 40 hours in custody before prosecutors decided they had acted in 'reasonable self-defense' and lifted the threat of charges.

Burglars who break into country homes can expect to be shot at by their victims, a judge warned yesterday.

Judge Michael Pert QC spoke out after a lawyer demanded leniency for a career criminal who he claimed had been blasted with a shotgun in 'a form of summary justice'.

The judge replied, 'If you burgle a house in the country where the householder owns a legally held shotgun that is the chance you take. You cannot come to court and ask for a lighter sentence because of it.'

Both men were out of prison on license when they struck at the Ferries' 200-year-old rented home.

Judge Pert backed householders' rights to defend their home from intruders, telling Mansell and O'Gorman: 'I make it plain that, in my judgment, being shot is not mitigation.

'You cannot come to court and ask for a lighter sentence because of it.'

He spoke out after Andrew Frymann, defending O'Gorman, suggested his client's 'near death experience' should be 'taken into consideration' by the judge when sentencing.

Mr. Frymann said O'Gorman had suffered serious facial injuries including permanent scarring. He added, 'He was shot – without any warning or foresight – in the face with a shotgun.

'This is a form of summary justice or punishment which I submit should be taken into consideration.'

Leicester Crown Court yesterday heard Mansell and O'Gorman fled empty-handed from the cottage and were arrested hours later when they went to hospital for treatment.

'Their injuries were clearly visible as they stood in the dock. Mansell – who has a tattoo reading 'Big Man' on his neck – wore his arm in a sling, and O'Gorman has a scar from his right eye to his ear.

Alan Murphy, prosecuting, said the Ferries were woken by the sound of breaking glass as the raiders forced their way into their home with a garden fork handle.

As they made their way downstairs, Mrs. Ferrie, the registered keeper of the shotgun, handed the weapon to her husband. Mr. Murphy said, 'Mr. Ferrie described seeing three men in the hall or kitchen wearing some form of face coverings.

'One of the men was reaching into a drawer that held a number of knives. As a result Mr. Ferrie fired his shotgun.'

Mr. Ferrie, 35, who owns a motor home repair business, then called the police, and he and his 43-year-old wife were arrested.

O'Gorman had 16 previous convictions involving 27 offences. He was on license at the time he broke into the cottage, having been released early from a 14-month prison sentence for dangerous driving.

Mansell has eight previous convictions involving 19 offences. He was freed on license following a conviction for causing grievous bodily harm.

Mansell and O'Gorman, both of Leicester, admitted to burglary with intent to steal.

Last night Mrs. Ferrie's mother, Hazel Towell, 63, said the couple had moved to Perth in Western Australia because they feared for their safety.

The retired cashier, from Burton, Staffordshire, added, 'They've moved as far away as possible.'

The fear was real enough for Andrew and Tracey to stay in a different hotel every night until they flew to Australia on Monday. They felt safer if they moved around.

Tory MP Alan Duncan spoke in defense of the Ferries, his constituents, while the couple was in custody. Yesterday he welcomed the judge's robust comments. 'Three cheers for the judge,' he said. 'Justice has been swift in this case and draws a clear distinction between the culprits and the victims.'

On Tuesday 18th September 2012 two Manchester Police Officers, Fiona Bone, 32, and her colleague Nicola Hughes, 23, were on a routine patrol in the Mottram district of Greater Manchester when they responded to reports of a house burglary on the city's Hattersley Estate. They had no way of knowing that this was not a routine call. Inside the house was one of the most wanted men in England. Shortly before 11 a.m., the pair, who like most UK Police Officers, were unarmed, arrived at the scene, a terraced house in Abbey Gardens. They were driving a marked Police Cruiser.

As they approached the house, Dale Cregan, aged 29, a man already on the run from police, after murdering another man and his son, suddenly emerged from the house. He was armed with a Glock pistol with an extended magazine. Without warning he opened fire. Both women were wearing body armor and Cregan's first 5 shots struck the officers chests but were stopped by the body armor. Cregan switched his aim and this time the bullets found their mark and Nicola fell forward. Cregan shot her 3 more times as she lay paralyzed. Fiona was the only officer armed, but she had only a taser.

She managed to pull her taser (stun gun) from its holder but was cut down in a hail of 24 bullets; one struck her in the head. As she fell the taser fired harmlessly into the ground. It was found next to her lifeless body. Cregan then threw a fragmentation hand grenade at the downed officers. Cregan had fired a total of 32 rounds. He then calmly walked away and got into a vehicle before driving to the police station.

Both women were fatally injured, Fiona dying at the scene while paramedics were unable to save her colleague, who died on the way to hospital.

A short time later the suspect Dale Cregan, walked into nearby Tameside police station and gave himself up. Police discovered that Cregan had made the initial call giving the name Adam Gantree and stating that someone had thrown a concrete slab through the back window. He had deliberately called the police in a bid to lure officers into a deadly ambush. Such is the state of Tony Blair's Gun free Britain in 2012.

Dale Cregan had been the subject of the biggest manhunt in Greater Manchester Police's history with officers offering a £50,000 reward for information leading to his capture. Greater Manchester Police had arrested Cregan on a charge of murder in June of 2012. Inexplicably they released him on bail and he subsequently absconded. He had been on the run since August, following the murder of David Short, 46, in a grenade attack on his home in the East Clayton district of Manchester. Two months earlier, he had gunned down Mr. Short's 23-year-old son, Mark, in a pub in Droylsden.

The murders inevitably sparked a debate about the routine arming of police officers and more direct questions were leveled at Sir Peter Fahy, Manchester's Chief Constable, as to whether female officers should have been attending an incident when the force's biggest manhunt was still underway. But Sir Peter insisted there had been no intelligence linking Cregan with the address. He told reporters

"We are passionate that the British style of policing is routinely unarmed policing. Sadly we know from the experience in America and other countries that having armed officers certainly does not mean that

police officers do not end up getting shot."

With due respect Sir Peter, American Police Officers are permitted to shoot back, a privilege denied the two female officers faced with a crazed killer, whose murderous mission the UK government had made so much easier.

In fact weapons and grenades are freely available in the UK on the black market. The dealings are said to be worth hundreds of thousands of pounds each year.

High-level criminals are now turning to grenades to beef up their lethal armory. The most commonly used are the Swiss-manufactured British Army-issue L109 and the Yugoslavian-made M75. In the UK in the three years up to March 2010, there were 14 grenade attacks in the UK – including seven in the North West in just 10 months. Weapons and grenades were often smuggled in from abroad, along with drugs. The EU open border policy makes it child's play, as there is lower security on the cross channel ferries that cross daily between France, and Belgium.

Day-trippers cross both ways and guns and weapons are often hidden in cars that are rarely checked unless the Customs officers spot something unusual.

Underworld armorers even sell gangs "assassin kits" – including a gun, silencer, and bullets for £300, ($500.00). They also rent handguns out for as little as £200, ($450.00). Many guns are hired out without the ammunition to brandish or threaten. But bullets – known as "food" in the underworld, are readily available at anything from £5 to £15 each depending on the caliber and quantity.

The Gun control lobbies are largely silent in the UK when incidents like this occur, but some newspapers are at last beginning to take notice. As an ex police Officer I can't help but wonder how many more officers have to be killed before some form of common sense emerges.

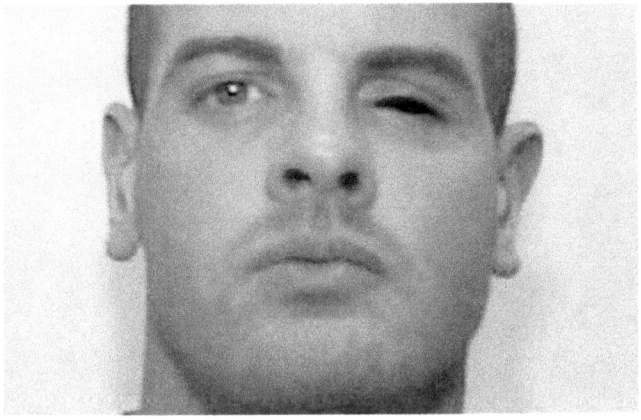

Police killer: Dale Cregan. He had lost his left eye in a gang fight before the incident.

WPC Fiona Bone (Left) and WPC Nicola Hughes unarmed victims of Dale Cregan

Andrew and Tracie Ferris: who used a legally held shotgun to defend themselves against home invaders. They were arrested by the police who eventually dropped charges. The wounded intruder sued them for putting him in fear of death.

The judge threw the case out, stating that, *"if you break into a farm in an isolated area, you should expect the owners to have a shotgun."*

Pressure from the left wing groups and gun ban brigade forced them to leave England.

Below, The Ferris Farmhouse

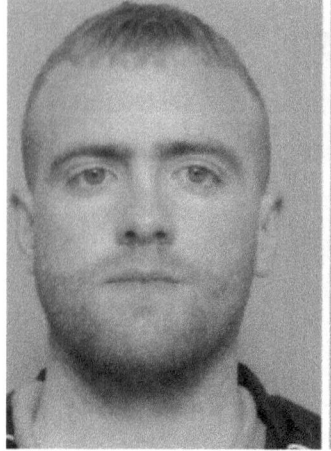

Police Mug shot of the Ferris home invaders;
Joshua O'Gorman and Daniel Mansell.

Dunblane Killer   Hungerford killer
Thomas Hamilton   Michael Ryan

The widespread illegal gun confiscation in New Orleans following Hurricane Katrina in 2005 cost the city dearly. It led to a change in the law, preventing the seizure of guns during a civil disaster. Some citizens guarded their shattered homes (above left) with stark warnings to looters. The press for once publicized the debacle caused by incompetent police and city officials (above right).

Above, the dome rescue center where disarmed survivors suffered rape and robbery, while the police failed to protect them.
Below, the author with his latest Winchester shotgun, a 12 gauge pump.

Chapter 6

How Strong Is the Second Amendment?

As previously stated, there are some major differences between Great Britain and the United States, the chief one of these is a little thing called The Constitution of The United States. This document written over two hundred years ago - ironically - to forge a nation's independence from Great Britain has stood the test of time. There can be little doubt that the Framers were well aware of the importance of getting it right, as we found out in the Supreme Court ruling on Heller v District of Columbia.

The law in the United States is based on English law. In particular the Supreme Court justices in the Heller ruling cited the Castle Doctrine and made reference to definitions in law. For those who are not familiar with law, I will explain.

Laws usually contain definitions of the terms used in that law.

For example, the term's people's rights and militia all have to be clearly defined; this is to make the intention of the lawmakers clear and un-ambiguous.

For example in the U.K. the term *theft*, as defined in the Theft Act of 1968, is defined as

"The dishonest appropriation of property, belonging to another, with the intention of permanently depriving the other of it."

This definition is used by U.K. officers when deciding the appropriate charge to bring against an offender, depending on the circumstances. If the definition does not fit, for example the offender took a car and drove it to another location, then left it undamaged. They could claim they had no intention to permanently deprive the owner of the car. Theft would not be the correct charge, and a different one, of *taking the vehicle without consent would be more appropriate.* Such is the world of lawmakers and judges. That is the way laws are written

Madison researched the Bill of Rights very thoroughly before presenting it to Congress.

The concerns of the colonist's, to be able to defend themselves were made very clear to him during this process. It is also clear that the Constitution could not have been passed without it. The Second Amendment establishes gun ownership as a right. It applies to both keeping (owning), and bearing (carrying for any purpose).

With this amendment as a cornerstone of the Constitution, Americans have retained their ownership of firearms, despite the technical improvements that have come since. The Supreme Court has ruled clearly that the term 'Arms' is not confined to one type or one caliber of weapon, in fact it is not confined to firearms at all. Arms are arms be they guns, swords or bows and arrows. Since the Bill of Rights became law, the country has remained one of the freest in the world.

The question of the Second Amendment was raised on many occasions. The first of which was *U.S. v. Cruikshank* 1876. This case involved members of the Ku Klux Klan and was more about depriving black citizens of their basic rights, such as freedom of assembly and to bear arms.

The court decided that neither the First nor Second Amendments applied to the States, but were limitations on Congress. Thus, the federal government had no power to correct these violations; rather, the citizens had to rely upon the police power of the states concerned for their protection from private individuals.

It is often said by the gun- control lobby that this case held that the Second Amendment does not grant a right to keep and bear arms. This is incorrect.

The case merely stated that neither the First nor the Second Amendment rights were granted or created by the Constitution; they existed *prior* to the Constitution.

Presser v. Illinois, 1886, ruled that the states had the right to strictly regulate private military groups and associations. It also reaffirmed the Cruikshank decision that the Second Amendment acts as a limitation upon the federal government, and not on the states. However, Presser also stated that setting the Second Amendment aside, the states could not prohibit the "people from keeping and bearing arms, so as to deprive the United States of their rightful resource for maintaining the public security..."

Miller v Texas 1894 Franklin Miller, convicted of murder, on appeal, claimed his Second and Fourth Amendment rights had been violated under the Fourteenth Amendment. The court upholding the conviction reaffirmed Cruikshank v. U.S. and stated *"And if the fourteenth amendment limited the power of the states as to such rights, as pertaining to citizens of the United States, we think it was fatal to this claim that it was not set up in the trial court."* In other words the court wouldn't even consider whether Miller's rights had been violated under the Fourteenth Amendment because he had not filed such a claim in his original trial.

U.S.A. v Miller 1939 Frank Layton and Jack Miller were charged with violating the 1934 National Firearms Act, which regulated and taxed the transfer of certain types of firearms, and that further, required the registration of such arms.

The *Miller* court ruled as follows:

1) The National Firearms Act was not an unconstitutional usurpation of police power reserved to the states.

2) "In the absence of evidence tending to show that possession or use of a 'shotgun having a barrel of less than 18 inches in length,' which is the subject of regulation and taxation by the National Firearms Act of June 26, 1934, has some reasonable relationship to the preservation or efficiency of a well-regulated militia, it cannot be said the Second Amendment to the Federal Constitution guarantees the right to keep and bear such an instrument, or that the statute violates such constitutional provision."

3) "It is not within judicial notice that a shotgun having a barrel of less than 18 inches in length is any part of the ordinary military equipment or that its use could contribute to the common defense."

4) "The Second Amendment must be interpreted and applied with a view to its purpose of rendering effective the Militia."

Regarding item 4) above, the *Miller* court defined the Militia in the following paragraphs.

The signification attributed to the term Militia appears from the debates in the Convention, the history and legislation of Colonies and States, and the writings of approved commentators.

These show plainly enough that the Militia comprised all males physically capable of acting in concert for the common defense. "A body of citizens enrolled for military discipline." And further, that ordinarily when called for service these men were expected to appear bearing arms supplied by themselves and of the kind in common use at the time.

I could not have put it better myself. The Supreme Court reversed the decision and remanded the case back to the district court, giving the defendants a chance to provide evidence that a short-barreled shotgun could contribute to "the efficiency of a well-regulated militia." (The Court was apparently unaware of the use of short-barreled shotguns in trench warfare during World War I.

It should of course be noted the Miller Court only required evidence that the weapon contribute to the efficiency of a well-regulated militia.

The Court never said the defendants had to belong to a well-regulated militia.

In other words, the *Miller* case interpreted the Second Amendment to mean one has the right to own militia type weapons.

States, however, continued to place restrictions on the Second Amendment with an apparent total inability to understand the phrase, shall not be infringed. The list of exceptions to the right to bear arms grew, alarmingly.

In the 1800s renowned frontier marshals such as Wyatt Earp and Bat Masterson happily enforced no- gun laws within city limits, (city ordinances), following rowdy mixtures of alcohol gambling and gunplay.

Weapons changed too. Single- action guns gave way to double- actions then semi- autos, and finally, fully automatic weapons. City mayors tried desperately to clean up the image of gangster- ridden Chicago and New York.

However there were at least some Americans who were prepared to fight for the Constitution and defy even the lawmakers.

156

One such patriot was Sheriff Richard Mack of Graham County Arizona, who took on the legislators and the Brady group by refusing to carry out the most restrictive provisions of the Brady Law. The requirement that the background checks be shifted from federal to local law enforcement was the line that Mack refused to cross.

He won and those parts of the Law were declared unconstitutional. Since that landmark case in 1995, Richard Mack has become a celebrity. He is much in demand as a speaker, and is likewise and understandably hated by the anti- gun liberal media.

The twentieth century has passed into history with the Second Amendment battered, but still essentially intact. The Supreme Court had looked at its various challenges and rejected any attempts to overturn it. The Bill of Rights still stands, as it always has. James Madison certainly knew his Job.

Chapter 7

The Introduction of Concealed Carry Legislation in the States

The problem facing lawmakers trying to regulate a population of armed citizens is that both the good and bad guys carry guns.

There was no specific law regarding how a gun could be carried. Pioneers and settlers routinely wore guns for convenience. They needed to be readily available. In towns and cities however where the threat was, at least, perceived to be less urgent, guns could be concealed in clothing and purses.

In England, Victorian ladies often carried muff pistols, small-caliber handguns that could easily be concealed in the fur hand muffs that were popular at the time. In the U.S.A., saloon girls often packed a small derringer in a stocking or purse, to deter the more persistent customers, while bankers and businessmen often preferred a small colt that could be carried unobtrusively inside a coat pocket or tucked in the waistband of their pants.

Laws prohibiting concealed- carrying of handguns without a permit are, in most of the United States, relatively recent. Some statutes that date from before the Civil War and concerned the carrying of concealed weapons simply made the practice illegal, even for peace officers. Faced with this, potentially severe threats, law enforcement personnel, were forced to assume everyone was a threat; lawmakers across America started looking afresh at the whole issue of concealed weapons.

During the 1920s and 1930s an act entitled *Uniform Act to Regulate the Sale and Possession of Firearms.* Was introduced and adopted by many states as well as by the National Conference of Commissioners on Uniform State Laws. It was also supported by the National Rifle Association.

This act, in essence, made it unlawful to carry concealed weapons without a license. One could have been forgiven for thinking that this was a move designed to ensure that owners who carried concealed were properly screened and trained, but in fact, the law was nothing of the sort, rather it stemmed from a desire by the authorities to control those who had access to guns.

Once legislation was in place, adopting states introduced amendments allowing for police and sheriffs departments to issue permits to persons on a discretionary basis. Without any standardized procedures in place, corruption and racism were rife. The underlying reasons were more likely to do with ensuring that the Second Amendment would never apply to any black American, immigrant, or catholic, rather than to keep guns out of criminal hands. This was especially true in the southern states where Confederate values, following the defeat of the South were undiminished.

Gradually states began to standardize the issue of concealed-carry permits. With strong support from the NRA, states began to issue permits to adult applicants with no criminal background. Broadly there were two types. Some States adopted a *'May Issue'* policy while others adopted a *'Shall Issue'* policy. The difference was not merely a grammatical one. Shall Issue states were required under their state constitutions or statues to issue permits to suitably qualified applicants. The sheriff's department had no authority to deny such applicants. In a May Issue state, the issue of permits was discretionary.

This anomaly caused a lot of concern, as politics again interfered with legislation. In May Issue states, gun-control advocates often blocked applications on frivolous grounds, many totally unconstitutional. Remedies were by way of long, expensive legal appeals through the court system, a path that the average gun owner could ill afford. Currently most of the high crimes, gun-control states are also the ones that have the 'May' issue permits. This is no coincidence.

Blatant abuses by states were taken up by the NRA and gradually, successful rulings in the both the Supreme and federal courts forced these states to comply with the Second Amendment, much to the fury of the gun- control lobby.

Each State has a different procedure for the issuance of concealed-carry permits. Some require the applicant to demonstrate accuracy and safety on a range, others merely an understanding of the law regarding the use of deadly force. Others e.g. Alaska and Arizona allow concealed carry with no permit requirement.

In 1987, Florida enacted a pioneering "Shall-Issue" right-to-carry law that has served as the model for the rest of the country.

The Florida law affirmed the right of a private citizen to carry a concealed gun. They eliminated the abuses so typical of "discretionary" right-to-carry laws that have resulted in gun permits being awarded arbitrarily to the political cronies of petty officials, limousine liberals, movie actors, athletes, and various other celebrity representatives of the rich and famous, while denying them to so-called "ordinary" citizens.

The Florida law made it crystal clear that any citizen with basic firearms training and a felony-free record would be issued a concealed-carry permit upon request, period.

Florida's landmark right-to-carry law was supported by the Florida Department of Law Enforcement, Florida Sheriffs Association, Florida Police Chiefs Association, and other law enforcement groups.

And more importantly, it was supported by Florida voters.

For the first five years after Florida passed its right-to-carry law, homicide rates in the U.S. soared. Florida's homicide rate fell a dramatic 23 percent. A few of the opponents of concealed- carry actually had the courage to admit they were wrong.

Thanks to the intensive lobbying efforts of the NRA, along with the tireless grassroots work of politically aware gun owners, thirty-three states now have Florida-style laws which require the prompt issuance to their citizens of legal permits to carry concealed weapons.

Well over half of the U.S. population, more than sixty percent of all handgun owners live in these Free states. Yet no more than one to five percent ever apply for such licenses.

Notwithstanding the fact that most people do not carry guns, the mere possibility that an intended target may be carrying has many would- be attacker thinking twice before attacking their victim. There is little doubt that if more publicity was given to attacks thwarted by an armed victim the crime rate would drop even further.

According to FBI, statistics states with shall issue right-to-carry laws have a twenty six percent lower total violent crime rate, a twenty percent lower homicide rate, a thirty nine percent lower robbery rate and a twenty two percent lower aggravated assault rate than those states that do not allow their citizens to legally carry guns for personal protection.

At the time of this writing (February of 2013), only one state, Illinois does not permit concealed carry and following legal action from the NRA, ILA. Has been forced to adopt CCW legislation.

Most States, though not all, recognize other states permits which allow greater freedom for an armed citizen to travel interstate and still have the ability to carry a gun for protection. The NRA is backing a bill to congress to compel all states to recognize other states permits. It remains to be seen if this is successful.

But, a word of caution here; just because the state you are visiting may recognize your permit, does not mean you do not need to know that states laws.

Some have restrictions on where the gun may be carried in a vehicle, or a requirement that you inform any police officer who stops you that you are a permit holder. Failure to comply could land you in court with your gun confiscated. So, check before travelling.

As a concealed carry instructor in Kentucky, I am often struck by the reasons applicants give for wanting to carry concealed. Most do feel that they will get greater security if they have immediate access to a firearm. Examples are female realtors who are concerned for their safety when showing empty homes to would- be buyers in rural locations, delivery drivers, or, just parents who feel they need to have the means to defend themselves and family should the need arise.

I recall one of my students, a delivery driver who had received a call from an anxious spouse one morning, reporting someone trying to break in. She had called 911. He was 30 miles from his home, but managed to arrive back there before the Sheriff's arrival. This made him acutely aware that the police cannot always be in a position to attend immediately, and that sometimes self - protection is down to the individual. Thankfully, his wife was not harmed, and both now are gun owners.

Carrying a concealed weapon is a decision that the individual gun- owner must make for himself. The decision to carry brings with it a number of other responsibilities not immediately realized by some applicants. Considering what they would do, or to be more precise, how they would react in an armed confrontation, is something that all concealed carry holders need to think on.

The first misconception that a new CCDW permit holder may have is that, like the heroic James Bond of literary fame, they have a license to kill. They do not.

The right to use deadly force is very conditional. If threatened, you can use your gun to stop the threat, and only that. Overstep the mark, by for instance shooting your attacker again while he or she is unconscious or disarmed, will probably get you a murder- one conviction.

This fact was clearly demonstrated when pharmacist Jerome Jay Ersland was convicted of first- degree murder in 2011.

Ersland was in his shop Reliable Discount Pharmacy, near SW 59 and Pennsylvania, in

Oklahoma City, Oklahoma, on May 19, 2009 when two men in ski masks threatened him and two other employees when they burst in demanding cash and drugs. The two robbers were aged fourteen and sixteen. Ersland pulled a gun and shot the sixteen year old, who dropped, unconscious to the floor with a head wound.

After emptying his gun at the fleeing second youth, Ersland returned to his store, retrieved a second weapon from a drawer, and shot the unconscious youth five more times.

Prosecutors at trial called the final shots an execution. Ersland said he was defending himself and two female co-workers. The jury disagreed, and Ersland went down for murder- one. In my opinion the jury got this one exactly right.

The decision of whether or not to shoot is usually a split- second one. The CCDW holder must assess the threat level, decide if it is high enough to warrant the shooting of a subject, and then has to bring his own weapon to bear on an armed suspect, who already probably has the advantage.

In that they has their weapon drawn and is already shooting, maybe directly at the permit holder. Nobody said it was an easy; ask any cop faced with a similar situation.

In Kentucky, the Department of Justice Criminal Training has issued its licensed concealed-carry instructors with a DVD prepared by its legal department. This DVD is required viewing at any CCDW course in the State.

This DVD contains an explanation of the law as regards to the carrying and use of deadly weapons in the State of Kentucky. I have lost count of the times I have viewed this film. And even I would have difficulty remembering every detail of it.

Lawyers impassionedly reading passages from law books at the camera hardly make for riveting Television. However the main points are well made and a good instructor will stop the DVD periodically to re-iterate certain points.

Unfortunately the inconvenient truth here is that it is solely the responsibility of the CCDW- holder to know the law and if they make a mistake. They alone will suffer the consequences.

I always tell my students that qualifying for the CCDW permit in Kentucky does not ensure that they will have the edge, should they be unlucky enough to be involved in a deadly encounter.

Practice at drawing, firing on the point and using the weak hand are all skills that an armed citizen needs to develop. And these are not usually taught on the course. Some shooting schools, including ours, do provide such extra practice and training as an option, but the old adage that practice makes perfect still rules. I am surprised that many have given little thought as to how they would react, both during, and after, the event.

CHAPTER 8

Are Armed Citizens a Real Deterrent?

So! A leading question for the people of America is simply: Do guns make people safer?

To answer that question with any degree of certainty, we need to go beyond the political spin, beyond the academic opinions and special interest groups. We need to base our opinion on cold- hard facts, not the opinion of a Brady group spokesperson, or for that matter, a local militia leader sporting an array of weaponry.

Facts, not opinions, are the only way to reach a clear and balanced position. What is needed is clear unbiased data, collected as to the occasions guns have been used in self-defense and the attitude of both victims and criminals to their use. And perhaps, most important the number of lives saved by a well aimed shot from the armed citizen or police officer.

The research done in the U.S.A. to support or reject gun- control has certainly been varied and has probably done little to further either sides cause.

In 1966, in response to an increase in rapes, the Orlando City Police Department introduced a gun-training program for women. The city experienced an eighty-eight percent drop in the rape rate the following year, even though rape had been on the increase in that city, in Florida, and in the United States as a whole at the time the program was introduced.

However, there were no similar drops in rape rates in the surrounding areas where no such programs were in place. And the drop in Orlando was far in excess of any one-year changes in previous rape rates. Similar results occurred in regard to other gun-training programs.

In 1978, a national survey found that seven per cent of households in America reported that a household member had used a handgun in self- defense against another person.

This figure did not include military or law enforcement incidents.

Seven years later, another survey, as carried out by an anti- gun organization, The National Alliance against Violence found a figure was six per cent.

It is officially estimated that between 1976 and 1981 there were 645,000 defensive uses of handguns by civilians, alone, per year. Firearms of all types are estimated to have been used by civilians for defensive purposes about 1,000,000 times a year during that time period. If law enforcement were required to record all such incidents and the FBI required to collate and publish them, I feel the case would be proven beyond all doubt. Of course the gun control lobby would, I am sure, vehemently oppose any such suggestion.

There is, however, no doubt that the people in this country feel that they need to possess guns to enable them to defend themselves. This is unsurprising in view of the knowledge that police response times are well short of what would be required to stop an attacker engaged in an assault, even if the victim had the chance to call.

This of course is in no way a reflection on the police.

It is blatantly obvious that officers cannot always be within one minute of a reported intruder or home invasion. In the rural areas of the country the response can be anything up to an hour.

Clearly the best option is to take steps to deal with the situation, as efficiently as possible, while awaiting police arrival. Remember, legally the police have no statutory duty to defend you. Conversely the sight of a targeted victim with a drawn gun has deterred many a criminal, but what of the other side? What do the criminals feel about their victims being able to defend themselves?

In 1993, The Department of Justice carried out a survey in an effort to find out what the criminal thought. The survey was carried out by two professors, James D. Wright and Peter H. Rossi. The survey was published in 1986, under the title *Armed and Considered Dangerous: a survey of felons and their firearms.* The academics interviewed over eighteen hundred prison inmates in ten states. The survey results proved bad news for the anti- gun lobby.

Fifty-seven percent of those felons agreed, "Most criminals are more worried about meeting an armed victim then they are about running into the police." Fifty-six percent agreed that no one is going to mess around with a victim when he knows they are armed with a gun. Seventy-four percent agreed that "One reason burglars avoid houses when people are at home is that they fear being shot." And fifty-eight percent agreed that, "a store owner who is known to keep a gun on the premises is not going to get robbed very often."

The felon's perception of the risk of encountering an armed civilian is worthy of further study. This attitude affects the felon's criminal behavior. The study found that forty percent of felons surveyed admitted that they had at one time or another decided not to commit a crime because they knew or believed that their intended victim carried a gun, powerful ammunition for the NRA and gun-rights groups.

The Police, NRA, and most gun training schools have known of the value of gun training for years.

So, what is the police view on all this?

Well! That depends on who you ask. But, it is telling that in the Heller, District of Columbia landmark case. The Law Enforcement Alliance of America filed an amicus brief in support of the plaintiff.

The LEAA is the nation's largest non-profit, non-partisan coalition of law enforcement professionals, crime victims, and concerned citizens united for justice (according to their website). This organization felt it necessary to stand up for the Second Amendment in supporting the case.

Their view was matched by several other police agencies, but it's only fair to say, was opposed by others.

In this country there is a different attitude to law enforcement compared with the United Kingdom. I say this without any implied or intended criticism.

The principal difference is Politics. In the U.K. Police officers are forbidden from taking an active part in politics as it is considered incompatible with their oaths to 'Carry *out the duties of constable without fear or favor, malice or ill will'*.

This oath is sworn by every police officer in front of a justice at their time of appointment.

The British public is aware of this and accepts that the rules put them above politics therefore each side of the political divide, accepts their decisions without too much argument.

In the U.S.A. county sheriffs are elected, and usually align with one or another of the political parties. In his book, '*The County Sherriff, Americas Last Hope*', Former Arizona sheriff Richard Mack, states that this system means the officers are more accountable to the people who elected them.

While this is undoubtedly true, my suspicion is that some sheriffs who align with left wing politicians are likely to be unsympathetic to gun- rights issues and this is reflected, in say, a refusal to approve a concealed carry license, or to confiscate guns for minor infractions. On a wider view, a lawman with shall we say strong views on illegal immigration may be less sympathetic to an illegal immigrant who is the victim of a crime.

It is therefore not surprising that law enforcement officials are divided on this matter. The question should be, in my opinion, not what a police officer personally thinks of a law, but how he applies that law; I always tried to put personal feelings aside, during my police career. I am sure the vast majority of officers over here have similar views.

What is important in my view, is that the general public. The American people have confidence in their legislators, in the laws made and the police officers who enforce them.

Police officers do not make the law they enforce it. If the lawmakers pass a law that is unconstitutional, such as the Brady Act, then the public and the police have every right to challenge it, as was the case of Sheriff Mack.

So to return to the question at the head of this chapter, is the armed citizen a deterrent? The evidence from both criminals and the police seems to confirm that they are.

The FB1 statistics for 2010 also do not make good reading for the anti-gun camp.

Considering five and ten year trends, the 2010 estimated violent crime total was 13.2 percent below the 2006, level and 13.4 percent below the 2001 level.

There were an estimated 403.6 violent crimes per 100,000 inhabitants in 2010. Also, aggravated assaults accounted for the highest number of violent crimes reported to law enforcement, at 62.5 percent. Robbery comprised 29.5 percent of violent crimes, forcible rape for 6.8 percent, and murder for 1.2 percent of estimated violent crimes in 2010.

Information collected in the same year regarding type- of- weapon showed that firearms were used in 67.5 percent of the nation's murders, 41.4 percent of robberies, and 20.6 percent of aggravated assaults. (Weapons data is not collected for forcible rape.) At the same time that firearms murders were dropping, gun sales were surging.

A rough guide to firearms sales can be had from the Bureau's background checks, required under the Brady Law. The data is far from conclusive, as it does not include personal face to face transactions, for example at gun shows, or transactions under

C&R procedures which do not require these checks. When you add an estimate covering these, the likely total firearm sales figure would be considerably higher.

In 2009, FBI background checks for gun purchases increased by thirty percent over the previous year, while firearms sales in large retail outlets increased by almost forty percent. The number of applications for concealed -carry permits jumped across the country as well.

Naturally, there is dispute over the significance of the surge in gun sales. The Brady Campaign to Prevent Gun Violence, for instance, say that gun ownership in America is actually declining. Their view is "While there are more people with concealed- carry permits and there has been an increase in gun sales, the research indicates overwhelmingly that the same people are simply buying more guns and that there has been a sharp decline in the percentage of Americans who own guns."

Brady Campaign spokesperson Caroline Brewer said, "So while there may be more guns, they are in the hands of a smaller percentage of Americans."

Well! Nice try Caroline, but I would dispute your findings, and you give little indication as to what research you are referring.

While the background checks will give a good guide to the number of guns each individual buys, they will not necessarily indicate the end user.

Guns that are resold or bought as gifts for family members for instance will not remain with the buyer; so it is hardly accurate to use such data in this way, a classic Brady spin that is all too common from the anti-gun movement, who these days find themselves very much on the defensive.

According to FBI data, California had the most gun murders in 2010 - 1,257, which is 69 percent of all murders in 2010. In fairness, California gun murders are still down by 8 percent from the previous year. This still makes California the most dangerous state to live in with respect to armed crime. The State also has the highest safety rating from the Brady Group. Need I say more?

With the Washington, D.C. figures now available for 2010 the news is even worse. Broken down by the firearms murder rate per 100,000 people, the District of Columbia is number one, with 16 firearms murders per 100,000 people. D.C. also topped the list of firearm robberies per 100,000 people with 255.98.

Yet, D.C. has, arguably, has the tightest gun laws in the country. Although an outright ban on handguns was struck down by the Supreme Court in 2008, legislators have ensured that the new regulations for obtaining a registered handgun would be anything but easy.

One of the frequent arguments I heard in the U.K. against arming the police was that doing so would encourage every young felon to carry a gun, in response.

Well, the British police still do not carry guns and the government over there banned them and announced the problem is solved.

Well! Good result, assuming you can ignore the massive rise in gun- crime and the death rate that followed in its wake.

Police officers in Britain are facing armed criminals daily and unlike their U.S. counterparts they do not have the means to return fire, unless you count pepper sprays and tasers. Incidentally, there are moves underway in UK to ban tasers because they may injure or kill an assailant who is trying to kill or maim the officer. Honestly! I am not making this up.

"Today, we need a nation of Minutemen, citizens who are not only prepared to take arms, but citizens who regard the preservation of freedom as the basic purpose of their daily life and who are willing to consciously work and sacrifice for that freedom."

-- John F. Kennedy

CHAPTER 9

Lessons from New Orleans

"When a strong man, fully armed, guards his house, his possessions are safe."
- Luke 11:21

On August 29th, 2005, Hurricane Katrina slammed into the Gulf Coast and the city of New Orleans, Louisiana was right in its path. The storm surges overwhelmed the city's inadequate levees and flooded eighty percent of the city.

The unfolding disaster filled the headlines for weeks and stories of courage and self-sacrifice where commonplace. Like other cities in the U.S.A. New Orleans had a large proportion of gun- owners, and many of them posted notices on their shattered properties stating that looters would face an armed response. (More than a few were less polite.)

The city authorities, alarmed at a number of shooting incidents ordered a policy of gun-confiscation.

Weapons found in abandoned houses by law enforcement personnel were seized, allegedly for safekeeping.

All refugees were searched, and disarmed by police, before being allowed into rescue centers. At the time, Police Superintendant Eddie Compass made the announcement, "Only law enforcement is allowed to have weapons. We are going to take all of the weapons."

At the time, the implications of this statement were not realized, it was understood, and implied, that these weapons would be returned to their owners following the disaster.

The reason for this action was given as public safety, following a number of incidents of shootings at police officers and emergency workers. The confiscation was enacted under statutory Louisiana law which states that *after the declaration of a state of emergency by the governor, the chief law enforcement officer of the political sub division affected by the proclamation may promulgate regulating and controlling the possession, storage, display, sale, transport, and use of firearms, other dangerous weapons, and ammunition.*

All fair enough, but the law was limited. It did not, and could not, cover total confiscation, as to do so breached the states own constitutional version of the Second Amendment, which reads:

"The right of each citizen to keep and bear arms shall not be abridged, but this provision shall not prevent the passage of laws to prohibit the carrying of weapons concealed on the person."

So, at this stage, the authorities were on shaky legal ground to say the least. As reports flooded in about house- to- house searches and guns being taken from the survivors of the disaster, authorities were quick to announce that all guns would be returned to their rightful owners once the disaster had passed.

This assurance, heavily reported by the media, went some way to allaying fears but that was soon to change, as reports began to flood in of incidents where defenseless citizens were being robbed, raped, and burglarized, even while in the supposed protection of rescue centers.

Clearly something had gone very wrong.

Two weeks after the seizures had begun the NRA president spoke out against the policy, pointing out that the conditions in New Orleans were exactly the conditions where the Second Amendment was intended to allow citizens to protect themselves.

On September 23rd, 2005 the NRA, and another group, The Second Amendment Foundation filed for a temporary restraining order against the city and its mayor.

On September 24th, 2005 The U.S. District Court for the Eastern District of Louisiana issued a temporary restraining order barring any further gun confiscations and ordering the return of lawfully owned firearms to their owners. This order was simply ignored by the authorities, who continued the policy of disarming residents while acknowledging that the police were overwhelmed. Yet again, politics had overruled legal judgments, and the mayor and police chief had set themselves above the law.

As a result, On March 1, 2006, the NRA filed a motion for contempt against the city of New Orleans, its mayor, and the chief of police for failure to comply with the order.

By this time stories were circulating wildly of multiple abuses of Second Amendment rights.

Refugees in the superdome gave interviews stating that they were systematically abused and in some cases raped while police and officials stood by, unwilling, or unable to intervene.

On March 15th, 2006, lawyers from both sides reached an agreement in the case of *NRA v. Mayor Ray Nagin*, which was pending before a federal court. In the resulting agreement the city of New Orleans finally admitted that it held a number of confiscated firearms, and the Property and Evidence Division of the New Orleans Police Department agreed to return the firearms to their owners on request and proof of ownership, or affidavit.

However, in the chaos and destruction following Katrina many homeowners had lost everything, including the paperwork that would have proven ownership. The majority of the guns were never returned, and Police Department continued to refuse to return weapons.

One elderly owner turned up with his address, full details of the weapon, and even the gun's holster with the serial number stamped on it. The gun was a family heirloom. It made no difference, and the gun, as far as I am aware was never returned, even though the police had the weapon and the address from where it was taken, and ownership could easily have been proven.

This case and thousands like, it showed that the mayor and police chief were acting out of political motives, and had abandoned all pretence of serving and protecting the residents of that shattered city.

President Bush was under attack from the left- wing media over his response to the disaster, and in these years following 9/11, most were out to blame the president for almost everything,

However, there were also stories of people fighting back, defending their homes, and reclaiming the streets, which were abandoned by the city authorities.

In the city of Algiers, on the south side of the river, dozens of neighbors in one part of that city formed themselves into a militia.

After a car jacking and an attack on a home by looters, they shared firearms, took turns on patrol, and guarded the elderly. Although the initial looting had resulted in a gun battle, once the patrols began, the militia never had to fire a shot.

 While in the Garden District of New Orleans, one of the city's top tourist attractions, armed citizens on patrol quelled the unrest. Nightly, the media toured flooded areas showing defiant armed homeowners standing or sitting outside their houses, with homemade signs that made it clear what would happen to anyone trying to loot their home.

Clearly, the situation that occurred in New Orleans should never be allowed to be repeated. The law needed to be clarified and made unambiguous, so that even the most corrupt anti- gun mayor or police chief could never again so blatantly disregard the U.S. Constitution.

In June of 2006, Louisiana Governor Kathleen Blanco signed the NRA-backed law, forbidding the confiscation of firearms from law-abiding citizens during declared emergencies. Similar legislation had already been adopted in nine other states.

On October 4, 2006, President George W. Bush signed into law the NRA-backed Disaster Recovery Personal Protection Act of 2006, incorporated into the Department of Homeland Security Appropriations bill.

This legislation prohibits the confiscation of legal firearms from citizens during states of emergency by any agent of the federal government or anyone receiving federal funds (effectively, any federal, state, or local governmental entity), introduced in Congress, by then Representative and now Governor Bobby Jindal and Senator David Vitter, both of Louisiana. The bill enjoyed broad bipartisan support. It passed the House of Representatives by a margin of 322-99 and the Senate by 84-16 before becoming law.

There are definitely lessons to be learned from the chaotic events of New Orleans. The disaster showed that in times of natural or man made disasters the police and medical services could so be severely stretched they may well be overwhelmed. During those times, lawless elements will take advantage of conditions to prey upon their fellow human beings, and that the armed citizen will probably be the only defense available.

Although this has been touted for years by the NRA, and equally dismissed by the Brady Group and similar groups, in New Orleans we saw with our own eyes that the gun banners had got it very, very wrong, and innocent people died as a result.

As the memories of Hurricane Katrina fade into history, and the gun-ban lobby prepare for another assault on the right to self-defense, we should remember this vivid example of a world where Americans, already battered and bloodied by one of nature's worst disasters. These people were further attacked so ruthlessly by the policies of an inept city mayor and by a police and National Guard who had no concerns about trashing the Constitution.

Debarred the Use of Arms, 2nd Edition

Chapter 10

The (Gun- Free) Killing Zones

"Then it occurred to me with sudden and utter clarity that, just a few months earlier, I had made the stupidest decision of my life: My gun was not in my purse any longer! I had done what most people do: I had rationalized that the chances of my needing it was slim, and the chances of getting caught with it somewhat higher. I had figured, Oh! What the odds that I'll need this thing in a crowded place in the middle of the day."
Suzanna Gratia Hupp. *From Luby's to the Legislature Privateer Publications*

There is nothing that gets the media more fired up about gun control than an unexplained mass shooting in a public area. As the body count rises and unfeeling reporters shove microphones into the faces of grieving relatives and shocked survivors, so the gun control lobby goes into overdrive.

Virginia Tech, Columbine, Jonesboro, and Tucson; these locations bring to mind the same nightmare visions of carnage that, Hungerford and Dunblane do in the United Kingdom. The lone gunman who walks through a crowded school or shopping mall, picking targets at random in a seemingly mindless orgy of savagery. In such conditions, as in war, it is usual that truth is often the first casualty.

In Tucson, CNN confidently announced that Congresswoman Gabrielle Giffords had been assassinated by an armed gunman. Of course the brave lady survived the assassin's bullet, but it still took several hours for CNN to correct the error.

I noted that media coverage of that tragic event differed sharply depending on the news outlets bias. Some reported that Congresswoman Giffords was a supporter of the Second Amendment. Certainly, her campaign website says Gifford is a longtime gun owner who joined an amicus brief in 2008 to ask the Supreme Court to uphold gun ownership rights in Washington, D.C.

Others ignored this and concentrated on a Sarah Palin campaign ad showing Giffords and several other democrats with cross hairs over them, designating the seats as targets for the GOP (failing of course to point out a similar ad earlier in the year from the DNC.)

In the U.K. the hysteria following Dunblane drowned out all voices of reason, and the facts of the cases were quickly replaced by speculation and demands that this must never happen again, until it does happen again and the circus repeats itself. In England, we have seen that a total handgun ban had no positive effect.

In the U.S.A. there is however, one law that has had a dramatic effect. It has actually pushed the body count into astronomical figures. Again our misguided Brady Group is largely responsible. The Gun-Free School Zones Act of 1990 was like most of the anti gun legislation, promoted as a sensible precautionary law to keep children and other vulnerable people safe from guns. Schools were made gun-free zones and teachers, pupils and criminals were told that they could not carry guns within, 1000 feet of those premises. (Anyone see a flaw in this program?)

Ok. So far, so good, teachers and most pupils complied. After the Supreme Court struck down the law as unconstitutional, Congress quickly re-worked it and in 1996, it once again became law.

No persons, including concealed-carry permit holders and teachers were permitted to have a gun on school premises. Thus, criminals were duly informed that no persons on these premises would have the means to defend themselves. The scene was set for absolute carnage.

So! Let's look at some of the more horrific incidents that have resulted from Brady's law.

On Monday, December 1st 1997, in the city of Paducah, Kentucky, Michael Carneal, aged fourteen yrs, walked into a student-led prayer meeting, and stood, head bowed carrying a rolled up blanket. As the prayers ended he produced A semi auto .22 pistol and began firing at random, killing three female students and wounding five others.

The unarmed leader of the prayer group ordered him to drop the weapon, and was ignored. The brave man then tackled the youth and brought him to the ground.

Shocked, police who attended found that, in addition to the .22 pistol the youthful killer had another pistol, two rifles, and two shotguns in the school, wrapped in the blanket.

Judged to be mentally ill Carneal is now serving life for murder.

On May 21st, 1998, two teenagers were killed and more than twenty people wounded when a teenage boy opened fire at a Thurston High School in Springfield, Oregon.

The killer in this case was also a young teenager. Kip Kinkel, aged fifteen was a very disturbed young man who had been suspended from school after a stolen handgun and ammunition had been found in his locker. He returned home and formulated a deadly plan.

At 3:30 p.m. on May 20th, Kinkel retrieved his Ruger rifle from his parents' bedroom, loaded it, and went to the kitchen, where he killed his father with a shot to the back of the head. He then waited patiently for his mother to come home.

About 6:00 p.m., as she walked up the stairs from the garage, Kinkel told her that he loved her, and shot her twice in the back of the head, three times in the face, and once in the heart. He then dragged his mother's body from the bottom of the stairs into the garage and dragged his father into the bathroom, where he locked the door. He then placed a white sheet over each of the bodies.

The following morning, Kinkel drove his mother's car to the high school. He wore a long trench coat to hide the four weapons he carried: a hunting knife, a 9 mm Glock pistol, the Ruger .22 rifle he'd used to kill his parents the night before and a Ruger .22 pistol. He was also carrying 1,127 rounds of ammunition. His intent was clear, to kill as many people as possible.

Entering the school's patio area and encountering two students, Kinkel fired two shots, one fatally wounding Ben Walker and the other wounding Ryan Atteberry. Kinkel went on to the school's cafeteria, and walking across it, fired the remaining forty eight rounds randomly from his rifle at the panicking students, wounding twenty four of them and killing 16-year-old Mikael Nicholauson.

Kinkel had fired a total of 50 rounds, accumulating 37 hits and two fatalities before he emptied the rifle's magazine.

Kinkel's rifle was now out of ammunition and he tried to reload, at this moment-wounded student Jacob Ryker tackled him. The unarmed student was assisted by several other students.

In reply, Kinkel drew the Glock and fired one shot before he was disarmed. The 9mm injured Ryker again as well as another student. The students restrained Kinkel until the police arrived and arrested him. Nicholauson died at the scene; Walker died after being transported to the hospital and kept on life support until his parents arrived. The other students, including Ryker, were also taken to the hospital with a variety of wounds. Ryker had a perforated lung, but made a full recovery. Because of the gun free policy, it was left to courageous unarmed students to tackle this deranged killer. We can only speculate as to the final death toll, had they not intervened.

The Thurston incident was not the worst incident by far but it was nevertheless a frightening precursor of what was to come.

In 1999, one of the worst massacres occurred at the Columbine High School in Littleton, Colorado. Two senior students, Eric Harris and Dylan Klebold, wearing trench coats and armed with a mixed variety of weapons, approached the school entrance of this designated gun-free-zone, The two were determined to kill as many people as possible, and had the firepower to do it. The weapons they had at their disposal were an Intratech TECH DC9 High point mod 995 carbine and 2 savage pump action shotguns and a sawn off shotgun.

There was one slim chance to avoid the coming massacre. It came in the form of a school officer, Deputy Gardener, who was first on the scene and came under fire from Eric Harris who turned his semi auto rifle on the officer firing ten shots at him before the rifle jammed. The deputy returned fire with his service issue handgun, momentarily checking Harris's fire.

However, the student cleared the jam and continued firing at the deputy before re-entering the school to continue his murder spree.

Deputy Gardener, now low on ammo, took cover while calling for back- up, which arrived in the form of Deputies Scott Taborsky and Paul Smoker.

On reaching the scene, Deputy Smoker saw Deputy Gardener with his pistol drawn at his vehicle, as one gunman appeared at a school window with a semi-automatic weapon and began shooting again. Smoker returned fire and the gunman disappeared. Inside the school, panic-stricken high school pupils tried to flee as the two teenagers walked down the hallway and into the library, laughing out loud and spraying bullets at pupils indiscriminately.

Sounds of gunfire, of bullets hitting metal lockers and windows, and the screams of the wounded and dying, were clearly audible to the helpless officers outside.

Students began to spill out of the school; some injured others in deep shock. When gunfire subsided, a police S.W.A.T. team stormed the building. They were greeted with a scene of absolute horror.

Bodies of students littered the hallway and library. In the library along with their victims, lay the bodies of the two gunmen.

They had simply run out of people to kill, and had turned their weapons on themselves. Twelve students and one teacher died that day and twenty-one others had suffered gunshot wounds.

The Columbine High School massacre, as it came to be known, was sadly not an isolated incident. Virginia Polytechnic Institute and State University, is located in Blacksburg, Va., southwest of Roanoke. Founded in 1872, Virginia Tech as it is more commonly known now has more than 25,000 full-time students attending eight colleges and graduate programs on its 2,600-acre campus. On April 16th, 2007, the worst school shooting in U.S. history occurred. Again this was in a Brady-dedicated gun free zone.

Seung Hui Cho, a twenty three year old South Korean student had been upset over an issue with a female student. At 0715 hours (am) he entered the west Ambler Johnson Hall Dormitory, armed with a Glock Mod, 19, 9mm semi auto pistol and a. 22 Walther p22.

He found Emily J. Hilscher and Ryan C. 'Stack' Clark in a room on the 4th floor, and shot both dead at close range.

Police were later unable to establish a motive for the killings, though fellow students there suggested the killer had a fixation about Hilscher.

Following the shootings Seung, returned to his room at the University, and packed up a package of media items which he mailed to NBC News. Meanwhile police and University leaders were investigating the incident, but concluded it was an isolated one of a domestic nature.

They put out a person of interest bulletin on Hilscher's boyfriend who lived off-campus and later detained him for questioning. The University decided not to inform other students and not to evacuate the campus, a decision that would come back to haunt them in the years that followed.

After obtaining extra ammunition and reloading both guns, Seung left his room and went to Norris Hall building. Here, he used chains to secure classroom doors to prevent any escape attempts.

Then, with seventeen preloaded magazines, he walked around the building, firing at random.

Using both semi-auto weapons to devastating effect, entering room 207 where a German class was in progress, he fired at the class professor, hitting him in the head, and then opened fire on the stunned students. In all, 120 rounds were fired during the rampage. Thirty students died in the hail of fire and seventeen more were wounded.

As with Columbine, panic-.stricken students had to flee for their lives. With no arms available to the staff to defend themselves, they were literally sitting targets. The killing spree lasted 20 minutes.

Meanwhile, an assembled police S.W.A.T. team broke into the building using a shotgun breach round to overcome the chained doors. On entering, further shots were heard and the police quickly headed for the source. Knowing there was no escape, Seung, like the two killers at Columbine, put a gun to his head, and ended the horror.

At this point the reader may notice some patterns: all the killers were children under eighteen and pupils or ex-pupils at the schools. This disturbing trend is explored further in Governor Mike Huckabee's thoughtful book, *Kids who kill.*

Broadman and Holden 1988. In his book the governor and co-author Dr. George Grant, argue that violent video games are one of the root causes of such behavior.

This view is further strengthened by other researchers, notably, celebrated West Point Psychology Professor Lt. Col. Dave Grossman who provides compelling evidence in his best selling book *On Combat. Warrior Science Publications.* I heartily recommend both books to anyone seriously interested in the mindset of the mass killer.

Four years after the horror at Virginia Tech, I had the privilege of conducting a basic handgun course at our shooting facility in Jeffersonville, Kentucky. One of the students was a survivor of the massacre. During a break between lessons, I asked her why she had taken the course. Her reply was uncompromising:

"I never again want to be in a position that I am unable to defend myself."

I could continue relating numerous other incidents of shootings that occurred in gun-free zones. There is certainly a wealth to choose from.

Most shootings in the U.S. involving more than three victims have occurred in such places. The gun-free killing zones do not end with schools and colleges. In 1993, the newly elected anti gun President, William Clinton, issued regulations that effectively gave terrorists a real gift.

A total ban on servicemen and women carrying personal firearms on base was made, making it all but impossible for base commanders to issue soldiers with weapons for self-protection. Military police can still carry firearms, but the war in the gulf has meant they that are stretched inadequately thin.

The terrorist groups were well aware of Clinton's law.

On November 5th, 2009, at Fort Hood on the outskirts of Killen Texas, another shooting in another gun free zone shocked America. A U.S. born officer, in the US Army, Major Malik Hasan, whose family hailed from Palestine, walked into a medical centre on the base armed with 2 handguns.

Hasan, a medical officer, gave no warning and allegedly called out "Allahu Akbar"[1] (God is Great) before opening fire with one of the guns a semi automatic pistol on a group of US soldiers who were receiving medical check ups prior to deployment.

The soldiers were of course unarmed, thanks to the Clinton passed law. As a result thirteen of our brave soldiers died and thirty-one were wounded before civilian police officers who were attached to the army were able to reach the scene and return fire, bringing the crazed Muslim officer down.

The reason for the rampage was linked to the war on terror, but there is little doubt that the knowledge that none of his victims would be armed made his attack easier and more deadly.

The wife of one of the soldiers shot at Fort Hood understands all too well. In an interview on CNN following the shooting, CNN anchor, John Roberts asked Mandy Foster, the wife of a soldier awaiting deployment, how she felt about her husband's upcoming deployment to Afghanistan. Ms. Foster pulled no punches. She responded:

*"At least he's safe there, and he can fire
back, right?"*

Right on Ms. Foster, only in the Brady gun-
free killing zones are you forbidden to
defend yourself.

Congress has now enacted the 2011 National
Defense Authorization Act (NDAA), which
includes several provisions developed by
NRA-ILA and supported by pro-Second
Amendment lawmakers. The law will
provide practical benefits to gun owners
while generating revenue for military bases.
Most important, it will protect the privacy
and Second Amendment rights of gun-
owning military personnel and their
families, as well as those of civilian
employees of the Department of Defense.

First, the Act tackles the problem that the
NRA has complained about many times
over, military base or unit regulations that
ban or severely restrict gun possession by
service members or their families. It was
long overdue.

Take the regulations imposed at another
base, Fort Riley, Kansas.

The Fort Riley regulation required troops stationed there to register privately owned firearms kept off base, as well as firearms owned by their family members residing anywhere in Kansas. It also prohibited soldiers with right-to-carry permits from carrying guns for protection off base and off-duty. A restriction also seen imposed a few years ago on soldiers stationed in Alaska. Finally, the Fort Riley rules authorized unit commanders to set arbitrary limits on the caliber of firearms and ammunition their troops could privately own.

Apparently, the US military is also unclear on the meaning of the Second Amendment. Strange! That George Washington never seemed to have had this problem.

The law scrapping these dangerous regulations was welcome, if a little late, but it does not solve all the problems. Until some common sense is applied to laws rushed through by politically motivated politicians, there will still be tragedies like Fort Hood, Columbine, and Virginia Tech.

Incredibly, President of the Brady campaign, Paul Helmke, had no regrets over the law that allowed Major Hood to mow down so many of our brave servicemen. Saying publically that,

"This latest tragedy, at a heavily fortified Army base, ought to convince more Americans to reject the argument that the solution to gun violence is to arm more people with more guns in more places."

One is left wondering how many innocent victims have to die in these killing zones before he and the Brady group are finally satisfied.

I do not blame Helmke personally. He is, after all, just a shallow, misguided activist who has, under the First Amendment, the right to any opinion, No matter how ludicrous.

The real blame lies with politicians and lawmakers who cheerfully put his bizarre ideas into law. Putting politics and their own election chances above the safety of American citizens is totally unacceptable in any modern society. It should certainly have no place in the home of the free world.

I fear that in the future, there will be more killings and still more clamors from the liberal politicians to ban guns for all but the criminals, as a response.

This cycle cannot be allowed to continue as it did in the U.K. Failure to take action now will put all Americans at risk. For, the crazed killers will always seek the softest targets, and the Brady group seems determined to assist them as much as possible in their cause.

Thankfully the situation at Ford Hood may be not repeated.

But let's look at some other incidents, this time in places declared gun-free by state legislators. In these, the victims have decided that the fault lies with the legislators and not the killers, and more importantly they did something about it.

At lunchtime on October 16th ,1991, thirty two year old Suzanna Gratia was having a pleasant lunch with her parents in Luby's cafeteria in Killeen, Texas, when a pickup truck came crashing through the wall. A man leapt from the truck armed with two handguns, and plenty of spare magazines and started shooting everyone in sight.

Suzanna's father aged seventy-five yrs and a veteran of WW2, bravely charged at the gunman, who shot him in the chest. Gratia's mother broke free from her daughter and ran to her dying husband; she cradled his head as the gunman calmly put a gun to her head and shot her too. Suzanna's mother and father had both been shot dead in front of her. In all, twenty-four diners were killed before the killer turned the gun on himself.

Suzanna, like many of the diners there, were gun-owners, but at the time, Texas law prevented her from carrying it at that location, a restaurant that also served alcohol. So the .38 revolver that she relied on for protection was locked in her car.

She was not alone in being unarmed; many of the dead diners around her were also handgun owners and, in accordance with Texas law, their guns remained secure in their cars and therefore useless.

The only one armed in the diner that day was the gunman, who being a criminal did not need to obey the state statutes. This is the result when laws are rushed through without any thought as to the consequences.

Even before the Brady group had begun their usual clamor for more gun control, Suzanna had decided to fight back. Enraged at a law that prevented her from defending herself and her parents, she set out to change the laws that had caused so many deaths. She turned her anger on her legislators, who in her words had *"Legislated me out of the right to protect myself and my family."*

She joined the campaign for the right to carry-concealed weapons in Texas and she ran for the state legislature. She was successful on both counts, Representative (Gratia) Hupp served for 10 years in the state legislator and stood down in 2007 after deciding not to run again.

She was a leading voice in getting the concealed-carry laws adopted in Texas, and remains today a rock against any politician who is anti Second Amendment.

Unfortunately, Suzanna was not the only person who was forced to see a loved one die because of misguided anti- self- defense laws.

In 2009, another woman, Nikki Goeser, was victim to the same state laws that favored criminals over the law- abiding public.

On Thursday, April 2nd, 2009 Nikki and her husband were running a karaoke evening at Johnny's Sports Bar in South Nashville, Tennessee, when a man who had been stalking her for a while walked up to her. Her stalker, Hank Wise had been sending, what can be described as inappropriate emails to Nikki and was generally becoming a nuisance.

At the couple's request, the bar manager Jennifer King, asked Wise to leave the bar. Wise suddenly produced a. 45 pistol and shot Nikki's husband, Ben, in the head, then fired another five times into his chest at point blank range. The gunman, confident that no one would be armed, and therefore would not oppose him, tried to leave but was tackled and disarmed by several brave unarmed customers.

This is what Nikki said of the incident in a recent interview:

"On April 2, 2009, I was legislated out of my right to protect my husband, Ben Goeser, who was shot and killed in my presence at a restaurant. My permitted gun was locked in my vehicle just outside the front door, because

Tennessee state law told me I must.

"My stalker put six bullets in my husband. This did not happen out in a dark parking lot. It occurred right in the middle of a restaurant, and was carried out by someone that was carrying a gun illegally. I will never know if I could have saved Ben, because I never had the chance

The law that was in place at the time (no guns allowed in restaurants that serve alcohol) did nothing to stop my husband's murderer. But I, or another permit holder, might have had a chance."

Like Suzanna, Nikki was not prepared to let things be. She has campaigned tirelessly for change, and was eventually successful in getting the ban overturned, in spite of a veto by the Tennessee governor Philip Bredesen.

However, the change was appealed and the law struck down in November   2009. Nikki did not give up and finally got the legislation through, despite every effort by the liberal legislators t kill it. Thanks to Nikki, Tennesseans finally have a legal right to defend themselves if caught in a similar situation.

The NRA and concealed-carry holders everywhere have pledged to continue the fight until all states are forced to enact similar legislation.

I am sure they will eventually win. With brave advocates like Nikki Goeser and Suzanna Gratia (Hupp) on their side, how could they possibly lose?

Nikki has continued to stand up for the right to defend herself, and is a frequent speaker at gun rights rallies across the country. I had the privilege of meeting her when we shared a platform at the Gun Rights Rally in Frankfort, Kentucky in 2010 and again in 2011. Her courage and resoluteness in the face of constant attacks by the anti-self-defense lobby is a true inspiration to all who are today, holding the line and demolishing the legislators' attempts to take away our rights to defend ourselves.

Two other case studies are worthy of mention here. Both occurred in fast food restaurants with a strict no-firearms-allowed- by- members- of- staff policy.

The so-called Wendy's massacre was a shooting spree that took place in a Wendy's restaurant at 40-12 Main Street in Flushing Queens in New York City on May 24, 2000. The killings were carried out by thirty-six year-old John Taylor, a former employee of the restaurant, and his accomplice Craig Godineaux.
The robbery they envisaged was carefully planned, as Taylor had the manager of the restaurant (who he knew) summon the entire staff to the basement on the pretense of having an important meeting.

The two armed killers herded all seven Wendy's employees into a walk-in refrigerator. Once in the basement, Taylor and Godineaux bound and gagged all of the employees at gunpoint, covered their heads with plastic bags and methodically shot each of them in the head at point blank range with a Bryco Jennings Model J38 .380 caliber pistol. All but two of the employees died. One of the survivors dialed 911 and police arrived to find the victims and discovered $2,400 missing from the safe.

New York law and Wendy's corporate policy had prohibited the victims from arming themselves.

Taylor was a former employee who had been dismissed for theft by the manager. Because of this he was familiar with the operation and layout of the restaurant. Both would also have been well aware of the corporate policy of Wendy's that employees could not carry weapons even if they had a permit.

Patrick Castro, twenty-four, was one of the survivors. Mr. Castro, an immigrant from Ecuador, had taken a job at the Wendy's restaurant only two weeks before the robbery and murders. After the shooting he awoke in a walk-in refrigerator, his head was covered in a plastic garbage bag, his eyes and mouth stuck shut with duct tape, and his wrists bound tightly together behind his back. He was surrounded by the bodies of his work colleagues.

Later at Taylor's trial Castro gave the following haunting testimony:

When I came to, I knew I was still in the walk-in refrigerator where the employees had been ordered to go after they were bound and gagged. As I became more alert, I felt a heavy weight bearing down on my knees, and I began to remember, things in vivid flashes of horror.

"There was a man with a gun, the "chunky man' Someone said, at one point, "There are no more bullets." There were two gunshots, so loud that my ears were ringing, and then the cashier screamed: "What happened? What happened?" Then another shot rang out and the cashier was silent.

"I wriggled my wrists free of the tape, peeled away the plastic from my head, ripped the tape off my eyes and mouth and peered out around me. I called out, "Is everybody O.K.?" As I saw the bodies on the floor. 'Is everybody O.K.?'

No one answered, and I soon realized that there was blood dripping from my face.

"What was the weight on your knees?" asked Daniel Saunders, an assistant district attorney.

''Ali'', referring to Ali Abidat, 40, a co-worker who had been killed. "I did not know it then, but I had been shot in my right cheek, just below my ear, and left for dead."

After Castro had freed himself, he heard a noise and feared the gunmen were still in the restaurant.

So he put his hands behind his back, replaced the bag over his head, and pulled Mr. Abidat's body back onto his knees, then he laid still.

"I was thinking this guy was going to come back and finish me off," he said.

After waiting a few minutes, Castro heard another noise. This time, he saw that it was Mr. Johnson, another employee also inside the refrigerator, who looked, Mr. Castro said, "like he'd been punched or beaten" ,but was "trying to smile" when he saw Mr. Castro was alive.

Castro was able to carry Mr. Johnson out of the refrigerator and prop him up in a chair. He said he crawled "like a baby" around the basement, looking for signs of the gunmen, and when he saw none, made his way into the manager's office to call the police. He carried Mr. Johnson upstairs on his shoulders.

The killer John Taylor, was convicted, and sentenced to death. The sentence was overturned by the State Supreme Court and he is now serving life without the possibility of parole. (But as this in New York, Don't hold your breath).

It is of course a matter of conjecture as to whether the lives of anyone at Wendy's may have been saved, had an employee been armed. However Wendy's ensured that would not happen by their policy. As a result five people died.

Compare this incident with the second

This time, in North Carolina two men were shot and killed after police said they tried to rob a Pizza Hut in east Charlotte, NC. Two employees were in the back of the restaurant, cleaning, at about 11:15 p.m., when three men entered.

The armed men tried to force the employees into the business' cooler when one of the employees fired his personal gun at the suspects. The employee, who said he had been robbed twice on the job, shot and killed two of the suspects after he said they told him to raise his shirt, which was where his .25 Raven pistol was hidden.

At least two of the suspects had been carrying handguns. The suspects ordered the two employees into the cooler, and for some reason, at least one of the suspects began beating a Pizza Hut employee.

The second employee pulled out his own handgun and began shooting.

When police and paramedics arrived, they found two suspects on the floor, shot to death. The other suspect had run off. One investigator said told the press the following morning that it is possible the third suspect was wounded by the employee.

"We found some other evidence in the area of the business and are looking into that," he said. Investigators appeared to be looking for a possible trail of blood around the front of the restaurant to the side of the building. No customers were in the restaurant at the time of the incident.

Police said they found two handguns near the dead suspects. The media reported at the time that Kristin Young, a spokeswoman for Medic, North Carolina's Emergency Medical Service, had said the injured employee was taken to Carolinas Medical Center with injuries that were not life threatening. Investigators are questioning the employee who fired the shots who was not named but is a former deputy sheriff. He was not charged in relation to the shooting.

However Pizza hut did act. They dismissed the employee for having a gun on company property which is against their policy. It seems to me as if this company as well as Wendy's and several others, have simply put politics above the safety of their own staff. As a result they have put their lives at risk.

"But if someone has a gun and is trying to kill you, it would be reasonable to shoot back with your own gun."

The Dalai Lama

Note.

On March, 3rd, 2008 in West Palm Beach Florida, another Wendy's was the scene of a shooting that left 1 dead and 5 wounded and the shooter then shot himself. Conclusion! Gun free zones are killing zones, pure and simple.

Chapter 11

What is the Brady Battle Plan?

Having seen the way that the Gun Control Network operated in the U.K. and the way it used manipulation, falsehoods, and scare tactics to achieve its aim, I have a pretty good idea of the likely strategy that will be used in the U.S.A.

The Brady Group is using very similar methods and arguments here. The G.C.N. was established in the United Kingdom in the wake of the horrific murders in Dunblane. It was set up by a group that included academics, lawyers, and the parents of victims killed in Hungerford and Dunblane. As stated earlier in the book, they had a great advantage in that the country was still reeling from the latter. They scored a number of successes.

Firstly, they were instrumental in getting the Firearms Consultative Committee disbanded. They had to do this to effectively silence the voice of the gun-rights groups.

The F.C.C. was statutorily constituted to give advice to the Home Secretary about firearms matters and had been instrumental in the gradual easing of regulations and the certification procedures for shooters. It consisted of representatives of all the various shooting organizations and the police, as well as the Gun Control Network.

The G.C.N. campaigned for the abolition of the F.C.C. or its radical reconstitution. Their stated aim was to ensure that, if it continued to exist, it should represent the interests of victims, the medical profession, community groups and the wider public, not just the police and the shooters. It follows therefore that the abolition of the F.C.C. was essential to silence the gun lobby, at least at the government level. Following its disbandment the F.C.C. was replaced by a two-tier Firearms Advisory Committee.

In a written statement Home Office minister Caroline Flint, said the main committee would be made up of twenty-one members, "to be drawn in equal measure from shooting interests, law enforcement regulation, and organizations and community groups with an interest in the social consequences of firearms use and misuse."

It will be supported by a technical sub-committee with twelve to fifteen members "drawn principally from representatives of law enforcement bodies and shooting organizations with knowledge of firearms matters."

The main committee would "advise the Home Office on the law and policy on firearms, having regard to the need to maintain public safety and prevent criminal misuse, taking into account the interests of legitimate shooters and the efficient administration of controls."

In effect the new body was nothing of the sort, although one of its members on the shooting side was the largest shooting organization in the UK. The British Association for Shooting and Conservation or BASC for short.

Christopher Graffius, its Director of communications said at the time,

"BASC welcomes the recognition of the need to take account of legitimate shotgun and firearm users. As the largest shooting organisation in the UK, BASC expects to be represented on both committees, as we were on their predecessor.

It is important that the public perception that inner-city gun crime can be tackled by restrictions on lawful gun owners is broken down. Legal shooting sports and lawfully held guns have not contributed to the rise in armed crime in this country."

These comments were not widely reported however, outside the shooting fraternity. The G.C.N. continued its letter-writing campaign spreading alarm and suspicion to the U.K. population. This tactic worked well in the U.K.; it is unclear of how effective it will be in the U.S.A. However, a clue as to the sort of tactics likely to be used in the U.S.A. can be had from the following sample letter put out by them to their supporters.

(I have not altered or shortened it in any way. I am more than happy to credit the letter to them.)

"WE SUGGEST YOU HANDWRITE YOUR LETTER AND MAKE IT AS PERSONAL AS YOU CAN

TO COUNCILLOR (NAME)

Dear Mr/Ms/Mrs..............

Gun Control/ Combined Cadet Forces

I am writing to express my support for further gun controls and to urge the council to take what action it can to reduce the opportunities for shooting in [your area].

I very much hope that the Education Committee will take the view that the introduction of CCFs in state schools is entirely unacceptable for the following reasons;

1. *Guns are dangerous weapons and have no place in educational establishments; children should be protected from guns not encouraged to develop an interest in them.*
2. *Arsenals of guns pose a quite unnecessary risk to the safety of children and teachers. They are susceptible to criminal attack and require a level of security that is inappropriate to a school.*

3.   *If the Ministry of Defence has public money to spend on encouraging discipline and teamwork in children and young people then it should transfer that money to schools to be used for more suitable extra curricular activities e.g. outward bound courses or community/environmental service.*

This is an issue about which parents all over the country feel very deeply. Guns are made for killing and do not belong in schools.

Yours sincerely   "

We have, of course, already seen similar letters and anti- gun views here in the U.S.A., from officials like Mayor Bloomberg and his Mayors against Illegal Guns group and the Brady Centre group. This is hardly surprising, as the G.C.N. have established links with many overseas groups including the Brady centre. But in the U.S.A. they have additional problems. The U.S. Constitution is one such problem (Britain doesn't have one).

The Dunblane shootings were exploited to the fullest extent by the G.C.N.

And they were well prepared. A massive publicity machine swung into action to ensure the Government was caught on the back foot, and the fact that a general election was imminent fueled the furor.

In the UK, the Conservative Party could be roughly equated to the Republicans in the U.S.A., Likewise the Labour Party, would find kindred spirits in the DNC.

The G.C.N. knew this and campaigned furiously for the Labour Party, as it was seen to be more in favor of a total ban. Candidates were questioned in all debates as to their views on gun control, with heavily loaded questions, such as, how can it be right to put our children in danger, just so you can play cowboys? "

With financial backing for the anti gun politicians, it was inevitable that Labour would win. The G.C.N. lost little time in calling in the debt. Do you think it would be different in the U.S.?

In the U.S.A. it is more likely to adopt a creeping strategy. My view is that first they will go for mandatory gun registration.

Once achieved, that database will be available to be used in any future gun confiscation law, exactly as it was in the UK,

Following that, the next target is likely to be, a selective banning of certain categories of weapons. The most likely target will be the so-called assault rifles, the AR15 and AK 47s. There are already moves in the liberal wing of the Democratic Party to re-instate the Clinton era assault weapons ban. Restrictions on magazine sizes and types of ammunition are also likely to be in the Brady playbook.

None of the above will be accepted by groups such as NRA, RKBA (Right to Keep and Bear Arms) and GOA (Gun Owners of America) as they blatantly breach the Second Amendment.

I am sure the Brady group will offer the well- worn argument that they are not trying to stop Americans from possessing guns for self-defense; they are just trying to keep us all safe.

However, make no mistake; preventing citizens from defending themselves is precisely what they are aiming for.

While it is true that the Second Amendment does not specify particular weapons, it does state unequivocally that the right to keep and bear arms shall not be infringed. It could be well argued that a ban on any weapon type is an infringement.

Another area likely to receive attention from The Brady Group is gun shows. Currently, face-to-face transactions do not require background checks, and this, according to Brady, is a serious loophole.

However, as anyone who has regularly attended a gun show will happily attest, almost half of the sellers are Federal Firearms License holders (FFL) and are compelled to comply with the Brady law anyway.

The 'loophole' issue is really a decoy. Face-to-face personal transactions are not subject to any such restrictions. Getting a regulation on the statute books to force gun show venders to carry out checks would almost certainly lead to a ban on all transactions outside the F.F.L. system.

If such restrictions ever become law, then America is in serious trouble.

It was inevitable that there will be another mass shooting in the U.S. in the future in a gun free zone, and by a deranged killer who is seeking his few minutes of fame. Such an event occurred at Sandy Hook Connecticut in December 2012. When such an event occurs, the gun control lobby always takes to the airwaves to condemn gun owners and groups like the N.R.A. Sandy Hook was no different. In fact they were on the bandstand even before the tragic victims had been buried.

We need to be aware of this strategy and be ready to challenge it head on. If we fail then the U.S.A. will become a Utopia for the armed criminal and our law enforcement will be hard pressed to keep order.

Conclusions

Well! I have painted a pretty worrying scenario, haven't I? I make no apologies for doing so, but I am more than optimistic that there is hope on the horizon.

In early 2013 The Obama administration made its move following the Sandy Hook tragedy and attempted to pass its threatened gun-control agenda, at the time of writing for this edition they have not succeeded. This has led to anger from the far left and in particular the Brady Group. The reason is not hard to see.

The NRA has a strong membership, in both the Republican and Democratic Parties. Early in 2011, this was demonstrated when 51 members of the senate signed open letters from Senator Jerry Moran (Rep) and Senator John Tester (Dem), President Barak Obama, and his secretary of state, Hillary Clinton, stating that they would never vote for any legislation that would deprive the American people of the right to keep and bear arms. (See appendix 1)

As any vote would need the signature of two thirds of the Senate to pass any treaty, this sent an uncompromising message to an administration which many see as pro-gun control.

The letter was in response to a treaty negotiated by the United Nation on the Control of small arms. Its details were kept secret, but it was widely thought to impose registration and restrictions on the private ownership of firearms in the U.S.A. Secretary of State Hillary Clinton had already agreed to sign the U.N. treaty on behalf of the US, a move that to the NRA confirmed their worst fears. It was also widely reported that the president had personally assured Sara Brady that he would be introducing gun control under the radar.

This information, that seemed to originate from the Brady camp, was evidence that the group saw the Obama administration as their best chance to get gun-control legislation on the statute books. Since the events at Sandy Hook the pro and anti-gun camps have split into clearer defined lines. NRA membership has soared and the murder rate in Illinois continues to climb into the stratosphere.

The advocates of gun control now have had a harder time convincing a skeptical American public that disarming the people will make them safer.

Without the possibility of getting legislation through Congress, the President is unable to do much more to appease the Brady Group. I feel more optimistic now than when I first arrived in the U.S.A.

In January 2012 the NRA announced that 2012 would be the most important in the country's history, they cite many disagreements with the Obama administration and many of these fall outside the scope of this book.

The failed A.T.F. operation codenamed 'Fast and Furious' falls into this category, but there is a suspicion that the core of the operation was a desire to introduce national gun-registration, starting with the Border States, a serious charge if true.

As this whole matter is likely to be the subject of a protracted congressional investigation, I will not comment further, save to say that history has shown that governments who desire gun control often uses what could be termed 'smokescreen' tactic's to hide their true agenda. I saw this first hand in the U.K.

The next 2 years are pivotal in my opinion, and the 2012 general election did play a major role in which direction the United States heads.

This is true not only with regard to who won the presidency but which senators and lawmakers were elected, and what their views are on gun -control, At present Republicans firmly control the House and The Democrats the Senate. Any judges appointed by the President to the Supreme Court will also impact on the direction the country moves.

I hope and believe that any duly appointed and confirmed Supreme Court justice will base their decisions on constitutional law, and not political ideology.

In 1779, this country produced a radical document that laid down the blueprint for a new nation, conceived, as it states in the pledge of allegiance, as "one Nation under God with liberty and justice for all."

The United Kingdom followed a different path, and although in 2011 our two nations are more closely aligned, the differences are still apparent. No more so than in their respective approaches to the right to self-defense.

In his wonderful book, *"On Combat"* (*Warrior Science Publications*,) Lt. Col. Dave Grossman put it very well. In describing how 3 officers advanced on a shotgun-wielding madman who had already killed one person in a hotel.

"When the elevator doors whisked opened, the medics very wisely stayed behind, pressing themselves even harder against the elevators back wall, the cops on the other hand immediately exited the elevator and moved towards the killer.

Is there something wrong with these people?

No, there is something gloriously right with them. Because if we did not have warriors men and women willing to move toward the sounds of guns and confront evil ,within the span of a generation our civilization would no longer exist. "

Stephen Challis 2013.

Appendix 1

United States Senate
WASHINGTON, DC 20510

July 26, 2011

The Honorable Barack Obama
President
The White House
1600 Pennsylvania Avenue NW
Washington, DC 20500

The Honorable Hillary Clinton
Secretary of State
2201 C Street, NW
Washington, DC 20520

Dear President Obama and Secretary Clinton:

As staunch defenders of the rights of law-abiding Americans to keep and bear arms, we write regarding ongoing negotiations of the United Nations' Arms Trade Treaty, and to express concerns about any provisions that could potentially infringe upon those rights.

We support efforts to better regulate the international trade of conventional weapons, but such efforts must be done in a responsible manner. We should do everything we can to ensure these weapons do not end up in the hands of human rights abusers, terrorist groups, insurgents or organized criminal enterprises. Further, we should not allow the unregulated trade of these weapons to continue fueling conflict and instability in nations around the world. The profound human and economic toll from these conflicts is staggering and the subsequent impact on our nation's economic and security interests is increasing. The United States has adopted a rigorous system of arms export controls and it is time for other nations to abide by some of those same standards.

For the past few years, negotiations for the Arms Trade Treaty have progressed. As your Administration continues to engage in these negotiations, we strongly urge you to address a number of our concerns.

First and foremost, the Arms Trade Treaty must not in any way regulate the domestic manufacture, possession or sales of firearms or ammunition. Firearms possession is an individual right guaranteed by the Second Amendment and that cannot be subordinated, directly or indirectly, by any international treaty. We are encouraged that your administration is working to ensure that signatory countries will maintain the exclusive authority to regulate arms within their own borders. That must continue to be non-negotiable. We also oppose any inclusion of small arms, light weapons, ammunition or related materials that would make the Treaty overly broad and virtually unenforceable. Finally, the establishment of any sort of international gun registry that could impede upon the privacy rights of law-abiding gun owners is a non-starter.

243

.

<u>Appendix 2</u>

President Barack Obama
1600 Pennsylvania Avenue, NW
Washington, D.C. 20500

Secretary of State Hillary Clinton
2201 C St., NW
Washington, D.C. 20520

Dear President Obama and Secretary Clinton:

As defenders of the right of Americans to keep and bear arms, we write to express our grave concern about the dangers posed by the United Nations' Arms Trade Treaty. Our country's sovereignty and the constitutional protection of these individual freedoms must not be infringed.

In October of 2009 at the U.N. General Assembly, your administration voted for the U.S. to participate in negotiating this treaty. Preparatory committee meetings are now underway in anticipation of a conference in 2012 to finalize the treaty.

Based on the process to date, we are concerned that the Arms Trade Treaty poses dangers to rights protected under the Second Amendment for the following reasons.

First, while the 2009 resolution on the treaty acknowledged the existence of "national constitutional protections on private ownership," it placed the existence of these protections in the context of "the right of States to regulate internal transfers of arms and national ownership," implying that constitutional protections must be interpreted in the context of the broader power of the state to regulate. We are concerned both by the implications of the 2009 resolution and by the hostility to private firearms ownership manifested by similar resolutions in previous years—such as the 2008 resolution, which called for the "highest possible standards" of control.

Second, your Administration agreed to participate in the negotiation only if it "operates under the rule of consensus decision-making."

Given that the 2008 resolution on the treaty was adopted almost unanimously— with only the U.S. and Zimbabwe in opposition—it seems clear that there is a near-consensus on the requirement for the "highest possible standards," which will inevitably put severe pressure on the United States to compromise on important issues.

Third, U.N. member states regularly argue that no treaty controlling the transfer of arms internationally can be effective without controls on transfers inside member states. Any treaty resulting from the Arms Trade Treaty process that seeks in any way to regulate the domestic manufacture, assembly, possession, transfer, or purchase of firearms, ammunition, and related items would be completely unacceptable to us.

Fourth, reports from the 2010 Preparatory Meeting make it clear that many U.N. member states aim to craft an extremely broad treaty.

A declaration by Mexico and other Central and South American countries, for example, called for the treaty to cover "All types of conventional weapons (regardless of their purpose), including small arms and light weapons, ammunition, components, parts, technology and related materials." Such a broad treaty would be completely unenforceable, and would pose dangers to all U.S. businesses and individuals involved in any aspect of the firearms industry. At the 2010 Meeting, the U.S. representative twice expressed frustration with the wide-ranging and unrealistic scope of the projected treaty. We are concerned that these cautions will not be heeded, and that the Senate will eventually be called upon to consider a treaty that is so broad it cannot effectively be subject to our advice and consent.

Fifth, and finally, the underlying philosophy of the Arms Trade Treaty is that transfers to and from governments are presumptively legal, while transfers to non-state actors (such as terrorists and criminals) are, at best, problematic.

We agree that sales and transfers to criminals and terrorists are unacceptable, but we will oppose any treaty that places the burden of controlling crime and terrorism on law-abiding Americans, instead of where it belongs: on the culpable member states of the United Nations who have failed to take the necessary steps to block trafficking that is already illegal under existing laws and agreements.

As the treaty process continues, we strongly encourage your Administration to uphold our country's constitutional protections of civilian firearms ownership. These freedoms are not negotiable, and we will oppose ratification of an Arms Trade Treaty presented to the Senate that in any way restricts the rights of law-abiding U.S. citizens to manufacture, assemble, possess, transfer or purchase firearms, ammunition, and related items.

Appendix 3

Gun rights groups in the United States

1. The National Rifle Association, 11250 Waples Mill Road, Fairfax, VA 22030.

2. Gun owners of America, 8001 Forbes Place, Suite 102, Springfield, VA 22151

3. National Association for Gun Rights, P.O. Box 7002, Fredericksburg, VA 22401

4. United States Concealed Carry Association, 4466 Hwy P - Suite 204, Jackson, WI

5. Second Amendment Foundation, 12500 N.E. Tenth Place, Bellevue, WA 98005

6. Citizens Committee for the Right to Keep and Bear Arms (CCRKBA), Liberty Park 12500 N.E. Tenth Place, Bellevue, WA 98005

7. The Law Enforcement Alliance of America, Inc. (LEAA), 7700 Leesburg Pike, Suite 421, Falls Church, VA 22043

Anti Gun groups in the United States

1. The Brady Campaign to Prevent Gun Violence, 1225 Eye Street, NW, Suite 1100, Washington, DC 20005

2. Stop Handgun Violence One Bridge Street, Suite 300, Newton, MA 02458

3. The American Bar Association, 321 N Clark Street, Floor 16, Chicago, IL 60654

4. Legal community against Gun Violence, 268 Bush Street, # 555, San Francisco, CA 94104

5. Coalition to Stop Gun Violence, 1424 L Street NW, Suite 2-1, Washington, DC 20005

6. The Joyce Foundation, 70 West Madison Street, Suite 2750, Chicago, Illinois 60602

7. Violence Policy Centre, 1730 Rhode Island Avenue, NW Suite 1014, Washington, DC 20036

www.ingramcontent.com/pod-product-compliance
Lightning Source LLC
Chambersburg PA
CBHW071409170526
45165CB00001B/221